Lent and Easter Wisdom

from

THOMAS MERTON

LENT and EASTER WISDOM

from

THOMAS MERTON

Daily Scripture and Prayers Together
With Thomas Merton's Own Words

The Merton Institute for Contemplative Living
Compiled by Jonathan Montaldo

Liguori
LIGUORI, MISSOURI

Imprimi Potest:
Thomas D. Picton, C.Ss.R.
Provincial, Denver Province
The Redemptorists

Published by Liguori Publications
Liguori, Missouri
www.liguori.org

Library of Congress Cataloging-in-Publication Data

Lent and Easter wisdom from Thomas Merton : daily scripture and prayers together with Thomas Merton's own words / compiled by Jonathan Montaldo.—1st ed.
    p. cm.
ISBN 978-0-7648-1558-4
1. Lent—Prayer-books and devotions—English. 2. Easter—Prayer-books and devotions—English. 3. Catholic Church—Prayer-books and devotions—English. I. Montaldo, Jonathan. II. Merton, Thomas, 1915–1968.
    BX2170.L4L455 2007
    242'.34—dc22   2006032234

Liguori Publications, a nonprofit corporation, is an apostolate of the Redemptorists. To learn more about the Redemptorists, visit *Redemptorists.com.*

Printed in the United States of America
11 10 09 08 07 5 4 3 2 1
First edition

Contents

Preface

WITHIN THE LARGE, varied corpus of Cistercian monk Thomas Merton, a few of his books are overlooked. A gem that deserves review is *Seasons of Celebration*, a gathering of his meditations on the meaning of the sacred liturgy for the spiritual daily lives of Roman Catholic Christians. To highlight for readers the perennial value of these reflections, both for the quality of their spiritual instruction and for the beautifully expressed intuitions studded throughout, the readings in this text for Lent and Easter have been harvested from this one volume.

Merton wrote these collected fifteen essays between 1950 and 1964. His noninclusive language, although traditional in his time, grates on the ears of twenty-first–century readers, but the Merton Legacy Trust rightfully urges editors to publish his works as he wrote them. Merton needs no defense: he possessed one of the most inclusive minds and hearts among spiritual writers of his historical period. He always referred to the "human being" or "person" when he wrote generally of "man." If he could revise his work today, he would undoubtedly modify his language to more gracefully address everyone. Merton's writing always communicates his kinship, respect, and even love for all of us.

One of Thomas Merton's most consistent spiritual and literary exercises was writing journals. He believed that God was intimate to his most personal experiences, especially when he reflected upon and recorded them. And at the end of the day, Merton judged his journal writing to be his best. Thus it seems appropriate for this volume that the "Lenten Journal" portion of each day consist of suggestions to assist you in keeping a private journal of this season of your life in Christ. Whether your journal is a spiral notebook or pages bound in leather, you are invited to create a personal book of your journey through Lent and Easter (where everything is allowed to go) as you celebrate Eucharist, hear and do the word of God, and discern whatever wisdom you discover for your own life in the words of Thomas Merton.

JONATHAN MONTALDO
ASSOCIATE DIRECTOR
MERTON INSTITUTE FOR CONTEMPLATIVE LIVING

Introduction

MOST CATHOLICS SEEM to be aware that the forty-day period before the feast of Easter, Lent—which comes from the Anglo-Saxon word *lencten,* meaning "spring"—is a time marked by particular rituals, such as the reception of ashes on Ash Wednesday or the practice of fasting and almsgiving. What is the significance of these rituals, and how do we observe the Lenten season today?

A BRIEF HISTORY OF LENT

In the first three centuries of Christian experience, preparation for the Easter feast usually covered a period of one or two days, perhaps a week at the most. Saint Irenaeus of Lyons (ca. AD 140–202) even speaks of a *forty-hour* preparation for Easter.

The first reference to Lent as a period of forty days' preparation occurs in the teachings of the First Council of Nicaea in AD 325. By the end of the fourth century, a Lenten period of forty days was established and accepted.

In its early development, Lent quickly became associated with the sacrament of baptism, since Easter was the great baptismal feast. Those who were preparing to be baptized participated in the season of Lent in preparation for the reception of the sacrament of baptism. Eventually, those who were already baptized considered it important to join these candidates preparing for baptism in their preparations for Easter. The customs and practices of Lent, as we know them today, soon took hold.

LENT AS A JOURNEY

Lent is often portrayed as a journey, from one point in time to another point in time. The concept of journey is obvious for those experiencing the Rite of Christian Initiation of Adults (RCIA), a four-stage program of baptismal preparation that culminates during Lent and ends during the Easter Vigil.

But Lenten preparation is not limited to those who are preparing to be baptized and join the Church. For many Catholics, Lent is a journey that is measured from Ash Wednesday through Easter Sunday, but, more accurately, Lent is measured from Ash Wednesday to the beginning of the period known as the Triduum.

Triduum begins after the Mass on Holy Thursday, continues through Good Friday, and concludes with the Easter Vigil on Holy Saturday. Lent officially ends with the proclamation of the Exsultet, "Rejoice, O Heavenly Powers," during the Mass of Holy Saturday.

By whatever yardstick the journey is measured, it is not only the time that is important but the essential experiences of the journey that are necessary for a full appreciation of what is being celebrated.

The Lenten journey is also a process of spiritual growth and, as such, presumes movement from one state of being to another state. For example, some people may find themselves troubled and anxious at the beginning of Lent as a result of a life choice or an unanswered question, and, at the end of Lent, they may fully expect a sense of conversion, a sense of peace, or perhaps simply understanding and acceptance. Therefore, Lent is a movement from one point of view to another or, perhaps, from one interpretation of life to a different interpretation.

Scripture, psalms, prayers, rituals, practices, and penance are the components of the Lenten journey. Each component, tried and tested by years of tradition, is one of the "engines" that drives the season and which brings the weary spiritual traveler to the joys of Easter.

PENITENTIAL NATURE OF LENT

A popular understanding of Lent is that it is a penitential period during which people attempt to become more sensitive to the role of sin in their lives. Lenten sermons will speak of personal sin, coming to an awareness of the sins of others and the effect such sin might have, and, finally, the sin that can be found within our larger society and culture. Awareness of sin, however, is balanced by an emphasis on the love and acceptance that God still has for humanity, despite the sinful condition in which we still find ourselves.

The practice of meditation of the passion of the Lord, his suffering, and his death is also seen as part of the penitential experience of Lent. There is also a traditional concern for the reception of the sacrament of reconciliation during Lent. Originally, the sacrament of reconciliation was celebrated before Lent began; the penance was imposed on Ash Wednesday, and performed during the entire forty-day period.

SUMMONS TO PENITENTIAL LIVING

"Jesus came to Galilee, proclaiming the good news of God, and saying, 'The time is fulfilled, and the kingdom of God has come near; repent, and believe in the good news'" (Mark 1:14–15). This call to conversion announces the solemn opening of Lent. Participants are marked with ashes, and the words "Repent, and believe in the good news" are prayed. This blessing is understood as a personal acceptance of the desire to take on the life of penance for the sake of the gospel.

The example of Jesus in the desert for forty days—a time during which he fasted and prayed—is imitated. It is time to center attention on conversion. During Lent, the expectation is to examine our lives and, through the practice of prayer, fasting, and works of charity, seeks to conform our lives to Christ's. For some, this conversion will be a turning from sin to grace. For others, it will be a gracious turning toward the mystery of God in Christ. Whatever the pattern chosen by a particular pilgrim for an observance of Lent, it is hoped that this book will provide a useful support in the effort.

PART I

~~~~~~

READINGS *for* LENT

Ash Wednesday

LENT IS OUR "HOLY SPRING"

*E*ven the darkest moments of the liturgy are filled with joy, and Ash Wednesday, the beginning of the Lenten fast, is a day of happiness, a Christian feast. It cannot be otherwise, as it forms part of the great Easter cycle.

The Paschal Mystery is above all the mystery of life in which the Church, by celebrating the death and resurrection of Christ, enters into the Kingdom of Life which He has established once for all by His definitive victory over sin and death. We must remember the original meaning of Lent, as the *ver sacrum*, the Church's "holy spring" in which the catechumens were prepared for their baptism, and public penitents were made ready by penance for their restoration to the sacramental life in a communion with the rest of the Church. Lent is then not a season of punishment so much as one of healing.

THOMAS MERTON, *SEASONS OF CELEBRATION*, 113

A Season of Celebration

So if anyone is in Christ, there is a new creation: everything old has passed away; see, everything has become new! All this is from God, who reconciled us to himself through Christ, and has given us the ministry of reconciliation; that is, in Christ God was reconciling the world to himself.…So we are ambassadors for Christ…we entreat you on behalf of Christ, be reconciled to God. For our sake he made him to be sin who knew no sin, so that in him we might become the righteousness of God.

As we work together with him, we urge you also not to accept the grace of God in vain. For he says,
"At an acceptable time I have listened to you,
and on a day of salvation I have helped you."
See, now is the acceptable time; see, now is the day of salvation!

2 Corinthians 5:17—6:2

Prayer

With faith in your resurrection, with hope in your power that undoes every death, I lift up my heart with love for you. Send forth your Holy Spirit who makes me more deeply your disciple. Crossing the threshold of this holy season, I renew my gratitude for the gift of being alive. On this Holy Wednesday, my forehead smeared with ashes, I accept my own death as holy: you have sanctified it. I offer my life and my death in thanksgiving to you, Jesus, the Christ, my Savior and my God.

Lenten Journal

However you write in your Lent and Easter journal, be truthful to your own experience. The question proposed for each day is only suggestive. Give your heart and mind free range. A first question: In what ways do you consider Lent to be a "season of celebration"?

DAY 2

Thursday After Ash Wednesday

A SORROW THAT BRINGS JOY

*C*ompunction is a baptism of sorrow, in which the tears of the penitent are a psychological but also deeply religious purification, preparing and disposing him for the sacramental waters of baptism or for the sacrament of penance. Such sorrow brings joy because it is at once a mature acknowledgment of guilt and the acceptance of its full consequences: hence it implies a religious and moral adjustment to reality, the acceptance of one's actual condition. The acceptance of reality is always a liberation from the burden of illusion that we strive to justify by our errors and our sins. Compunction is a necessary sorrow, but it is followed by joy and relief because it wins for us one of the greatest blessings: the light of truth and the grace of humility. The tears of the Christian penitent are real tears, but they bring joy.

THOMAS MERTON, *SEASONS OF CELEBRATION,* 115–116

Choosing to Live

See, I have set before you today life and prosperity, death and adversity. If you obey the commandments of the LORD your God that I am commanding you today, by loving the LORD your God, walking in his ways, and observing his commandments, decrees, and ordinances, then you shall live and become numerous, and the LORD your God will bless you in the land that you are entering to possess. But if your heart turns away and you do not hear, but are led astray to bow down to other gods and serve them, I declare to you today that you shall perish; you shall not live long in the land that you are crossing the Jordan to enter and possess. I call heaven and earth to witness against you today that I have set before you life and death, blessings and curses. Choose life so that you and your descendants may live, loving the LORD your God, obeying him, and holding fast to him; for that means life to you and length of days, so that you may live in the land that the LORD swore to give to your ancestors, to Abraham, to Isaac, and to Jacob.

DEUTERONOMY 30:15–20

Prayer

My God, you have created me not to die for you but to live for you. You would not wish me blind to my destiny but to accept my life with eyes open to the possibilities of loving you and those intimates with whom I share my life. Open my eyes to my true destiny: to know you through the Son whom you have sent to teach me what I must do to be fully human. I must love you with my whole heart and love my neighbors as I love myself.

Lenten Journal

What are the illusions in my life that I accept as my reality?

DAY 3

Friday After Ash Wednesday

TRUSTING IN THE LORD'S MERCY

𝒾t is necessary that at the beginning of this fast, the Lord should show Himself to us in His mercy. The purpose of Lent is not only expiation, to satisfy the divine justice, but above all a preparation to rejoice in His love. And this preparation consists in receiving the gift of His mercy—a gift which we receive insofar as we open our hearts to it, casting out what cannot remain in the same room with mercy.

Now one of the things we must cast out first of all is fear. Fear narrows the little entrance of our heart. It shrinks up our capacity to love. It freezes up our power to give ourselves. If we were terrified of God as an inexorable judge, we would not confidently await His mercy, or approach Him trustfully in prayer. Our peace and our joy in Lent are a guarantee of grace.

THOMAS MERTON, *SEASONS OF CELEBRATION*, 116–117

Fasting by Being Merciful

> *Look, you fast only to quarrel and to fight,*
>   *and to strike with a wicked fist.*
> *Such fasting as you do today*
>   *will not make your voice heard on high.*
> *Is such the fast that I choose,*
>   *a day to humble oneself?*
> *Is it to bow down the head like a bulrush,*
>   *and to lie in sackcloth and ashes?*
> *Will you call this a fast,*
>   *a day acceptable to the LORD?*
>
> *Is not this the fast that I choose:*
>   *to loose the bonds of injustice,*
>   *to undo the thongs of the yoke,*
> *to let the oppressed go free,*
>   *and to break every yoke?*

ISAIAH 58:4–6

Prayer

The ears of my heart are opened to hear your commands. Teach me your ways. Teach me to be a disciple of Jesus by becoming a sign of mercy to my neighbors. Help me to accept their weaknesses as I accept my own. Teach me to understand that we are all sinners, groping our way toward you in a desert of forces arranged against us. Let nothing in me separate myself from my neighbors. There is one path toward you, that of mercy, and we must all be united and walk it.

Lenten Journal

How are fear and mercy factors in my relationship with God?

Saturday After Ash Wednesday

FASTING

*F*asting is not merely a natural and ethical discipline for the Christian. It is true that St. Paul evokes the classic comparison of the athlete in training, but the purpose of the Christian fast is not simply to tone up the system, to take off useless fat, and get the body as well as the soul in trim for Easter. The religious meaning of the Lenten fast is deeper than that. Our fasting is to be seen in the context of life and death, and St. Paul made clear that he brought his body into subjection not merely for the good of the soul, but that the whole man might not be "cast away."… [Fasting] has a part in the work of salvation, and therein the Paschal mystery. The Christian must deny himself, whether by fasting or some other way, in order to make clear his participation in the mystery of our burial with Christ in order to rise with Him to a new life.

THOMAS MERTON, *SEASONS OF CELEBRATION*, 121–122

FASTING FROM MALICIOUS SPEECH

If you remove the yoke from among you,
the pointing of the finger, the speaking of evil,
if you offer your food to the hungry
and satisfy the needs of the afflicted,
then your light shall rise in the darkness,
and your gloom be like the noonday.
The LORD will guide you continually,
and satisfy your needs in parched places,
and make your bones strong;
and you shall be like a watered garden,
like a spring of water,
whose waters never fail.
Your ancient ruins shall be rebuilt;
you shall raise up the foundations of many generations;
you shall be called the repairer of the breach,
the restorer of streets to live in.

ISAIAH 58:9B–12

PRAYER

Remove from my heart its malicious tongue that does not speak of peace but only of war and hate. Let me recognize by your grace and teaching the sins of my mouth, the harm I do so casually by my malicious words. Let me fast this Lent from all talk that puts down my neighbor, reviles my perceived enemies, and creates division instead of community. Lord, make my mouth an instrument of your peace.

LENTEN JOURNAL

How can you "fast" from thoughts and speech that harm others, the community, and yourself?

First Sunday in Lent

THE FATHER'S LOVE

*T*he Church's belief in Christ is not a mere static assent to His historical existence, but a dynamic participation in the great cycle of actions that manifest in the world the love of the Father for the ones He has called to union with Himself, in his beloved Son. It is not simply that we are "saved," and that the Father remits the debt contracted by our sins, but that we are loved by the Father, and loved by Him insofar as we believe that He has sent His Son, and has called Him back into heaven after having given all power into His hands.

In the liturgical year, the Church sees and acclaims this action of the Father who so loved the world that He gave His only begotten Son for the salvation of men.

THOMAS MERTON, *SEASONS OF CELEBRATION*, 54–55

FASTING IN IMITATION OF CHRIST

Jesus, full of the Holy Spirit, returned from the Jordan and was led by the Spirit in the wilderness, where for forty days he was tempted by the devil. He ate nothing at all during those days, and when they were over, he was famished. The devil said to him, "If you are the Son of God, command this stone to become a loaf of bread." Jesus answered him, "It is written, 'One does not live by bread alone.'"

LUKE 4:1–4

PRAYER

Lord Jesus, to be your disciple is to be without an insurance policy. You ask me to abandon a life that lives for bread alone. I sometimes doubt if there is any other. The challenge of your gospel intimidates me. Your courageous defiance of Satan, your fierce integrity, challenge my complacency. You have drawn me into your Lent and are making me afraid. Give me the courage to follow you.

LENTEN JOURNAL

What is "the world" that Jesus asks that you renounce?

DAY 6

Monday of the First Week of Lent

A PENITENT HEART

The Call to "do penance" is based not on the fact that penance will keep us in trim, but on the fact that "the Kingdom of Heaven is at hand." Our penance—*metanoia*—is our response to the proclamation of the Gospel message, the *Kerygma* which announces our salvation if we will hear God and harden not our hearts. The function of penance and self-denial is then contrition, or the "breaking up" of that hardness of heart which prevents us from understanding God's command to love, and from obeying it effectively.

THOMAS MERTON, *SEASONS OF CELEBRATION*, 130

Turning Toward Our Neighbors

"When the Son of Man comes in his glory, and all the angels with him, then he will sit on the throne of his glory. All the nations will be gathered before him, and he will separate people one from another as a shepherd separates the sheep from the goats, and he will put the sheep at his right hand and the goats at the left. Then the king will say to those at his right hand, 'Come, you that are blessed by my Father, inherit the kingdom prepared for you from the foundation of the world; for I was hungry and you gave me food, I was thirsty and you gave me something to drink, I was a stranger and you welcomed me, I was naked and you gave me clothing, I was sick and you took care of me, I was in prison and you visited me.' Then the righteous will answer him, 'Lord, when was it that we saw you hungry and gave you food, or thirsty and gave you something to drink? And when was it that we saw you a stranger and welcomed you, or naked and gave you clothing? And when was it that we saw you sick or in prison and visited you?' And the king will answer them, 'Truly I tell you, just as you did it to one of the least of these who are members of my family, you did it to me.'"

MATTHEW 25:31–40

Prayer

Let me see your face in every face I meet. Let me learn the intimate connection between love of you and compassion for all you have given me to be at one within their struggles and real suffering. Let me damp down my need to take and let my heart fill with the necessity to give, if I am to be your disciple.

Lenten Journal

What was your last act of "charity"? Why did you do it?

Tuesday of the First Week of Lent

CHRISTIAN SELF-DENIAL

*N*o one can really embrace the Christian asceticism mapped out in the New Testament unless he has some idea of the positive, constructive function of self-denial. The Holy Spirit never asks us to renounce anything without offering us something much higher and much more perfect in return....The function of self-denial is to lead to a positive increase of spiritual energy and life. The Christian dies, not merely in order to die but in order to live. And when he takes up his cross to follow Christ, the Christian realizes, or at least believes, that he is not going to die to anything but death. The Cross is the sign of Christ's victory over death. The Cross is the sign of life. It is the trellis upon which grows the Mystical Vine whose life is infinite joy and whose branches we are. If we want to share the life of that Vine, we must grow on the same trellis and must suffer the same pruning.

THOMAS MERTON, *SEASONS OF CELEBRATION*, 130–131

TURN FROM EVIL AND DO GOOD

Come, O children, listen to me;
I will teach you the fear of the LORD.
Which of you desires life,
and covets many days to enjoy good?
Keep your tongue from evil,
and your lips from speaking deceit.
Depart from evil, and do good;
seek peace, and pursue it.

The eyes of the LORD are on the righteous,
and his ears are open to their cry.

PSALM 34:11–15

PRAYER

I turn the tendrils of my heart to you today to embrace the trellis of the Cross. Raise me up toward more light that I might have life. Prune me for more life in you.

LENTEN JOURNAL

In what way could you consider yourself "a vine that God has pruned"?

DAY 8

Wednesday of the First Week of Lent

A BALANCED ASCETICISM

*C*hristian asceticism is remarkable above all for its balance, its sense of proportion. It does not overstress the negative side of the ascetic life, nor does it tend to flatter the ego by diminishing responsibilities or watering down the truth....It warns us that we must make an uncompromising break with the world and all it stands for, but it keeps encouraging us to understand that our existence in "the world" and in time becomes fruitful and meaningful in proportion as we are able to assume spiritual and Christian responsibility for our life, our work, and even for the world we live in. Thus Christian asceticism does not provide a flight from the world, a refuge from stress and the distractions of manifold wickedness. It enables us to enter into the confusion of the world bearing something of the light of Truth in our hearts, and capable of exercising something of the mysterious, transforming power of the Cross, of love and sacrifice.

THOMAS MERTON, *SEASONS OF CELEBRATION*, 131–132

Asceticism as Uncovering Our Inner Light

"No one after lighting a lamp puts it in a cellar, but on the lampstand so that those who enter may see the light. Your eye is the lamp of your body. If your eye is healthy, your whole body is full of light; but if it is not healthy, your body is full of darkness. Therefore consider whether the light in you is not darkness. If then your whole body is full of light, with no part of it in darkness, it will be as full of light as when a lamp gives you light with its rays."

LUKE 11:33–36

Prayer

Help me, Lord, to remove the beam in my eye that I might see more clearly the work of your hands in my neighbors' hearts. Dislodge the darkness in my heart and let the light of your presence, always within me, shine forth and bring the portion of your light that I possess to shine with yours for the sake of the world.

Lenten Journal

In what ways does your life lack "a sense of proportion"?

Thursday of the First Week of Lent

HARVESTING THE WORLD'S GOODS FOR GOD

*T*rue sanctity does not consist in trying to live without creatures. It consists in using the goods of life in order to do the will of God. It consists in using God's creation in such a way that everything we touch and see and use and love gives new glory to God. To be a saint means to pass through the world gathering fruits for heaven from every tree and reaping God's glory in every field. The saint is one who is in contact with God in every possible way, in every possible direction. He is united to God by the depths of his own being. He sees and touches God in everything and everyone around him. Everywhere he goes, the world rings and resounds (though silently) with the deep harmonies of God's glory.

THOMAS MERTON, *SEASONS OF CELEBRATION*, 137

Seek Good and You Shall Find It

"Ask, and it will be given to you; search, and you will find; knock, and the door will be opened for you. For everyone who asks receives, and everyone who searches finds, and for everyone who knocks, the door will be opened. Is there anyone among you who, if your child asks for bread, will give a stone? Or if the child asks for a fish, will give a snake? If you then, who are evil, know how to give good gifts to your children, how much more will your Father in heaven give good things to those who ask him!"

MATTHEW 7:7–11

Prayer

If I go to the sea, you are there. If I go to the forests, you are there. If I enter the city, you are there in everyone and everything I see. Open my eyes to your goodness that is everywhere around me. Give me a heart that delights in your infinite creativity.

Lenten Journal

How has God been good to you?

Friday of the First Week of Lent

THE GOAL OF ASCETICISM IS LIBERATION

*W*e cannot use created things for the glory of God unless we are in control of ourselves. We cannot be in control of ourselves if we are under the power of the desires and appetites and passions of the flesh. We cannot give ourselves to God if we do not belong to ourselves. And we do not belong to ourselves if we belong to our own ego.

The real purpose of Christian asceticism is then not to liberate the soul from the desires and needs of the body, but to bring the whole person into complete submission to God's will as expressed in the concrete demands of life in all its existential reality.

THOMAS MERTON, *SEASONS OF CELEBRATION*, 138

Turning Away From Our Sins

But if the wicked turn away from all their sins that they have committed and keep all my statutes and do what is lawful and right, they shall surely live; they shall not die. None of the transgressions that they have committed shall be remembered against them; for the righteousness that they have done they shall live. Have I any pleasure in the death of the wicked, says the LORD GOD, and not rather that they should turn from their ways and live? But when the righteous turn away from their righteousness and commit iniquity and do the same abominable things that the wicked do, shall they live? None of the righteous deeds that they have done shall be remembered; for the treachery of which they are guilty and the sin they have committed, they shall die.

EZEKIEL 18:21–24

Prayer

I shall understand your sacred mission to the world only by acknowledging my poverty, my imprisonment in a daily round of desires for empty things, my habitual blindness to who I truly am and who you truly are for me. Help me understand your work in me. You have come to liberate me just as I am. You love me just as I am. You will heal me just as I am. Today I know my sins and renounce them. I affirm my will to follow your way and be more truly your disciple.

Lenten Journal

What in your life do you find "unacceptable"? How does the "unacceptable" in your life relate to the injunction "Find God in all things"?

DAY 11

Saturday of the First Week of Lent

AN ORDERED ASCETICISM

*W*hatever may be the mode and measure of self-denial that God asks of us (and this is a matter that cannot really be decided without prayer and spiritual direction), all Christian asceticism is characterized by wholeness and by balance. Christ admits of no division. He who is not with Jesus is against Him....God asks us to give Him everything. But we have already said what that means: using all creatures for God alone. Consequently our asceticism must always be balanced. The true ascetic is not one who never relaxes, but one who relaxes at the right time and in the right measure, who orders his whole life, under the direct guidance of the Holy Spirit, so that he works when God wants him to work, rests when God wants him to rest and prays constantly through it all by a simple and loving gaze that keeps his heart and mind united with the indwelling Spirit.

THOMAS MERTON, *SEASONS OF CELEBRATION*, 141

LOVE YOUR ENEMIES

"You have heard that it was said, 'You shall love your neighbor and hate your enemy.' But I say to you, Love your enemies and pray for those who persecute you, so that you may be children of your Father in heaven; for he makes his sun rise on the evil and on the good, and sends rain on the righteous and on the unrighteous. For if you love those who love you, what reward do you have? Do not even the tax collectors do the same? And if you greet only your brothers and sisters, what more are you doing than others? Do not even the Gentiles do the same? Be perfect, therefore, as your heavenly Father is perfect."

MATTHEW 5:43–48

PRAYER

Order my disordered heart. Let me see in whoever is enemy and stranger to me the other half of myself that I refuse to embrace. Loving Spirit, perfect the image of your love in me every day. Create an inclusive heart within me. Let my heart become peaceful. May I bring peace wherever I go and to whomever I encounter.

LENTEN JOURNAL

Does "asceticism" (renouncing some comforts of life and practicing self-denial) have any role in your life?

Second Sunday of Lent

GATHERING TOGETHER TO MEET CHRIST

*L*iturgy is a *work* in which the Church collaborates with the divine Redeemer, renewing on her altars the sacred mysteries which are the life and salvation of mankind, uttering again the life-giving words that are capable of saving and transforming our souls, blessing again the sick and the possessed, and preaching His Gospel to the poor.

In the liturgy, then, the Church would have us realize that we meet the same Christ who went about everywhere doing good, and who is still present in the midst of us wherever two or three are gathered together in His name. And we meet Him by sharing in His life and His redemption. We meet Christ in order to *be* Christ and, with Him, save the world.

THOMAS MERTON, *SEASONS OF CELEBRATION,* 55

AWAKENING TO THE LORD'S GLORY

Now about eight days after these sayings Jesus took with him Peter and John and James, and went up on the mountain to pray. And while he was praying, the appearance of his face changed, and his clothes became dazzling white. Suddenly they saw two men, Moses and Elijah, talking to him. They appeared in glory and were speaking of his departure, which he was about to accomplish at Jerusalem. Now Peter and his companions were weighed down with sleep; but since they had stayed awake, they saw his glory and the two men who stood with him. Just as they were leaving him, Peter said to Jesus, "Master, it is good for us to be here; let us make three dwellings—one for you, one for Moses, and one for Elijah"—not knowing what he said. While he was saying this, a cloud came and overshadowed them; and they were terrified as they entered the cloud. Then from the cloud came a voice that said, "This is my Son, my Chosen; listen to him!" When the voice had spoken, Jesus was found alone. And they kept silent and in those days told no one any of the things they had seen.

LUKE 9:28–36

PRAYER

Awaken all of us who gather in your name, Lord, to the power of your death and rising from the dead. Allow us to rise from the sleep of our daily cares to the glory of your transfiguration, the light of your Father shining in you for us. Allow us to see how gathering in your name is to experience paradise.

LENTEN JOURNAL

What do you love about celebrating the liturgy with your faith community?

░░░ DAY 13 ░░░

Monday in the Second Week of Lent

OUR FEAR OF GENUINE FREEDOM

*I*f individualism and subjectivism are so widely suspect among us, there is perhaps a very good reason for it. We live in a climate of individualism. But our individualism is in decay. Our tradition of freedom which, as a matter of fact, is rooted in a deeply Christian soil, and which in itself is worthy of the highest respect and loyalty, has begun to lose its genuine vitality. It is becoming more and more a verbal convention rather than a spiritual conviction. The tendency to substitute words about freedom for the reality of freedom itself has brought us to a state of ambivalent spiritual servitude. The noise with which we protest our love of freedom tends to be proportionate to our actual fear of genuine freedom, and our guilt at our unconscious refusal to pay the price of freedom.

THOMAS MERTON, *SEASONS OF CELEBRATION*, 19–20

Free to Be Hungry for the Kingdom of Heaven

Then he looked up at his disciples and said:

"Blessed are you who are poor, for yours is the kingdom of God.

"Blessed are you who are hungry now, for you will be filled.

"Blessed are you who weep now, for you will laugh.

"Blessed are you when people hate you, and when they exclude you, revile you, and defame you on account of the Son of Man. Rejoice on that day and leap for joy, for surely your reward is great in heaven; for that is what their ancestors did to the prophets.

"But woe to you who are rich, for you have received your consolation.

"Woe to you who are full now, for you will be hungry.

"Woe to you who are laughing now, for you will mourn and weep.

"Woe to you when all speak well of you, for that is what their ancestors did to the false prophets."

LUKE 6:20–26

Prayer

You enjoin me to give up everything to follow you. You teach me that the price of genuine freedom is to become poor and hungry for the kingdom of heaven. Freedom for your disciples is freedom to do justice and liberate our neighbors, as we liberate ourselves, from whatever keeps us fettered in ignorance of your command to love our neighbors as ourselves.

Lenten Journal

What does spiritual freedom mean in your life? What is keeping you from being "free" to love God and serve your neighbor selflessly? More positively: how did you become "free to serve"?

Tuesday in the Second Week of Lent

The Illusion That We Are Free

*T*he illusory character of the freedom which we have tried to find in moral and psychological irresponsibility has become inescapable. Our abdication of responsibility is at the same time an abdication of liberty. The resolution to let "someone else," the anonymous forces of society, assume responsibility for everything means that we abdicate from public responsibility, from mature concern and even from spiritual life. We retire from the public realm of freedom into the private world of necessity, imagining that the escape from responsibility is an escape into freedom. On the contrary, it is, in Erich Fromm's words, an "escape from freedom." But when we turn over the running of our lives to anonymous forces, to "them" (whoever "they" may be, and nobody quite knows), what actually happens is that we fall under the tyranny of collective fantasies and delusions.

Thomas Merton, *Seasons of Celebration,* 20

DOING JUSTICE

Hear the word of the LORD,
  you rulers of Sodom!
Listen to the teaching of our God,
  you people of Gomorrah!...

Wash yourselves; make yourselves clean;
  remove the evil of your doings
  from before my eyes;
cease to do evil,
  learn to do good;
seek justice,
  rescue the oppressed,
defend the orphan,
  plead for the widow....

How the faithful city
  has become a whore!
  She that was full of justice,
righteousness lodged in her—
  but now murderers!
Your silver has become dross,
  your wine is mixed with water.
Your princes are rebels
  and companions of thieves.
Everyone loves a bribe
  and runs after gifts.
They do not defend the orphan,
  and the widow's cause does not come before them.

Therefore says the Sovereign, the LORD of hosts,
the Mighty One of Israel:
Ah, I will pour out my wrath on my enemies,
and avenge myself on my foes!
I will turn my hand against you;
I will smelt away your dross as with lye
and remove all your alloy.
And I will restore your judges as at the first,
and your counselors as at the beginning.
Afterward you shall be called the city of righteousness,
the faithful city.

Zion shall be redeemed by justice,
and those in her who repent, by righteousness.
But rebels and sinners shall be destroyed together,
and those who forsake the LORD shall be consumed.

ISAIAH 1:10, 16–17, 21–28

PRAYER

Save me, O God, from being a full participant in a society grown fat and rich on the backs of others. Take off my blinders so I may see the injustice and poverty everywhere around me. Help me to understand the need for a repentance that turns my heart to a loving and just relationship with everyone.

LENTEN JOURNAL

Have you turned over responsibility for your life to the influences of our culture? To whom and to what have you made yourself subservient?

DAY 15

Wednesday in the Second Week of Lent

THE ILLUSION OF INDIVIDUALITY

*W*e are beginning to understand that we live in a climate of all-embracing conformities. We have become mass-produced automatons. Our lives, our homes, our cities, our thoughts, or perhaps our lack of thoughts have all taken on an impersonal mask of resigned and monotonous sameness. We who once made such a cult of originality, experiment, personal commitment and individual creativity, now find ourselves among the least individual, the least original and the least personal of all the people on the face of the earth—not excluding the Russians. In this desperate situation, the ideal of individuality has not been laid aside. Rather it has taken on the features of an obsessive cult. People "express themselves" in ways that grow more and more frantic in proportion as they realize that the individuality and the distinctive difference they are attempting to express no longer exists. To adapt the old French proverb, the more we try to express our difference by "originality," the more we show that we are the same: *plus ça change, plus c'est la même chose.* There is nothing so monotonously unoriginal as the capricious eccentricities of atoms in a mass-society.

THOMAS MERTON, *SEASONS OF CELEBRATION,* 20–21

THE NEED FOR REFORMATION

The word that came to Jeremiah from the LORD: "Come, go down to the potter's house, and there I will let you hear my words." So I went down to the potter's house, and there he was working at his wheel. The vessel he was making of clay was spoiled in the potter's hand, and he reworked it into another vessel, as seemed good to him.

Then the word of the LORD came to me: Can I not do with you, O house of Israel, just as this potter has done? says the LORD. Just like the clay in the potter's hand, so are you in my hand, O house of Israel. At one moment I may declare concerning a nation or a kingdom, that I will pluck up and break down and destroy it, but if that nation, concerning which I have spoken, turns from its evil, I will change my mind about the disaster that I intended to bring on it. And at another moment I may declare concerning a nation or a kingdom that I will build and plant it, but if it does evil in my sight, not listening to my voice, then I will change my mind about the good that I had intended to do to it. Now, therefore, say to the people of Judah and the inhabitants of Jerusalem: Thus says the LORD: Look, I am a potter shaping evil against you and devising a plan against you. Turn now, all of you from your evil way, and amend your ways and your doings.

But they say, "It is no use! We will follow our own plans, and each of us will act according to the stubbornness of our evil will."

Therefore, thus says the LORD:
Ask among the nations:
Who has heard the like of this?

The virgin Israel has done
a most horrible thing.
Does the snow of Lebanon leave
the crags of Sirion?
Do the mountain waters run dry,
the cold flowing streams?
But my people have forgotten me,
they burn offerings to a delusion;
they have stumbled in their ways,
in the ancient roads,
and have gone into bypaths,
not the highway,
making their land a horror,
a thing to be hissed at forever.
All who pass by it are horrified
and shake their heads.
Like the wind from the east,
I will scatter them before the enemy.
I will show them my back, not my face,
in the day of their calamity.

JEREMIAH 18:1–17

PRAYER

I listen to the words of your prophets as they express in human terms the alienation we experience when we ignore your counsel and become self-centered, both as individuals and collectively. Lord, have mercy. Christ, have mercy. Lord, have mercy.

LENTEN JOURNAL

What might I do to close the distance between God and myself created by things I do or neglect to do that make me feel an absence of God in my life?

Thursday in the Second Week of Lent

CHRISTIAN PERSONALISM

What is the real root of personality in a man? It is obviously that which is *irreplaceable*, genuinely unique, on the deepest spiritual level. *Personalism* is the discovery, the *respect*, but not the *cult*, for this deep reality. Secular personalism is a...craze for individuality, a rage for self-manifestation in which the highest value is sought in the *recognition* by others of one's own uniqueness.

But the great paradox of Christian personalism is this: it consists in something more than bringing to light the unique and irreplaceable element in the individual Christian. On the contrary, Christian personalism does not require that the inmost secret of our being become manifest or public to all. We do not even have to see it clearly ourselves! We are more truly "Christian persons" when our inmost secret remains a mystery shared by ourselves and God, and communicated to others.

THOMAS MERTON, *SEASONS OF CELEBRATION*, 21–22

BARREN BUSHES

Thus says the LORD:
Cursed are those who trust in mere mortals,
*   and make mere flesh their strength,*
*   whose hearts turn away from the LORD.*
They shall be like a shrub in the desert,
*   and shall not see when relief comes.*
They shall live in the parched places of the wilderness,
*   in an uninhabited salt land.*
Blessed are those who trust in the LORD,
*   whose trust is the LORD.*
They shall be like a tree planted by water,
*   sending out its roots by the stream.*
It shall not fear when heat comes,
*   and its leaves shall stay green;*
in the year of drought it is not anxious,
*   and it does not cease to bear fruit....*
I the LORD test the mind
*   and search the heart,*
to give to all according to their ways,
*   according to the fruit of their doings.*

JEREMIAH 17:5–8, 10

PRAYER

Let me feel shame, Lord, for my sins, particularly ones based on injustice and unconcern. Let me know my heart as it is in your sight and in my neighbors' sight. Straighten the torturous paths of my heart.

LENTEN JOURNAL

Consider the "inmost secret" at the core of yourself that is shared with God and remains a mystery.

DAY 17

Friday in the Second Week of Lent

DISCOVERING OUR INMOST SELF

*C*hristian personalism does not root out the inner secret of the individual in order to put it on display in a spiritual beauty-contest. On the contrary, our growing awareness of our own personality enables us at the same time to divine and to respect the inner secret of our neighbor, our brothers and sisters in Christ. Christian personalism is, then, the sacramental sharing of the inner secret of personality in the mystery of love. This sharing demands full respect for the mystery of the person, whether it be our own person, or the person of our neighbor, or the infinite secret of God. In fact, Christian personalism is the discovery of one's own inmost self, and of the inmost self of one's neighbor, in the mystery of Christ: a discovery that respects the hiddenness and incommunicability of each one's personal secret, while paying tribute to his presence in the common celebration.

THOMAS MERTON, *SEASONS OF CELEBRATION*, 22

DOING JUSTICE AND PRAYING IN SECRET

"Beware of practicing your piety before others in order to be seen by them; for then you have no reward from your Father in heaven.

"So whenever you give alms, do not sound a trumpet before you, as the hypocrites do in the synagogues and in the streets, so that they may be praised by others. Truly I tell you, they have received their reward. But when you give alms, do not let your left hand know what your right hand is doing, so that your alms may be done in secret; and your Father who sees in secret will reward you.

"And whenever you pray, do not be like the hypocrites; for they love to stand and pray in the synagogues and at the street corners, so that they may be seen by others. Truly I tell you, they have received their reward. But whenever you pray, go into your room and shut the door and pray to your Father who is in secret; and your Father who sees in secret will reward you.

"When you are praying, do not heap up empty phrases as the Gentiles do; for they think that they will be heard because of their many words. Do not be like them, for your Father knows what you need before you ask him."

MATTHEW 6:1–8

PRAYER

My God, help me to see the mystery and beauty in every person and to respond with love and joy to your presence within them.

LENTEN JOURNAL

What do you know about yourself that you cannot communicate? What is your most personal, and thus perhaps your most beautiful, secret?

DAY 18

Saturday in the Second Week of Lent

FINDING OURSELVES IN PUBLIC WORSHIP

*N*ow it is precisely in the liturgy, the *public* prayer of the Christian Assembly, that the Christian discovers the secret of his own inviolable solitude, and learns to respect the solitude of his brother and sister while at the same time sharing it. This is not possible without the *public* celebration of the mysteries: public of course to the faithful assembly, though not to the uninitiated.

Christian persons find themselves and their brothers and sisters in the *communal celebration of the mystery of Christ.* But what is manifested, proclaimed, celebrated and consummated in the liturgy is not *my* personality or *your* personality: it is the personality of Christ the Lord, who, when two or three of us are gathered together in His Name, *is present in the midst of us.* This presence of Christ in the liturgical celebration leads to our discovery and declaration of our own secret and spiritual self.

THOMAS MERTON, *SEASONS OF CELEBRATION*, 22–23

FINDING OURSELVES FORGIVEN IN CHRIST

Who is a God like you, pardoning iniquity
and passing over the transgression
of the remnant of your possession?
He does not retain his anger forever,
because he delights in showing clemency.
He will again have compassion upon us;
he will tread our iniquities under foot.
You will cast all our sins
into the depths of the sea.
You will show faithfulness to Jacob
and unswerving loyalty to Abraham,
as you have sworn to our ancestors
from the days of old.

MICAH 7:18–20

PRAYER

I do not know myself outside of those who gather in your name to praise your sacred deeds for our salvation proclaimed in the gospel and celebrated in our Eucharist. Give me the grace to cleave myself to the assembly gathered by you. There is no salvation for me outside the presence of my brothers and sisters who together hear and do your word.

LENTEN JOURNAL

How do you understand Saint Paul's words: "I am yours, you are mine and we are Christ's"? Do you sense in this statement the essence of Christian spirituality?

DAY 19

Third Sunday of Lent

THE ETERNAL PRESENT OF CHRIST'S ENERGY

*I*n every liturgical mystery we have this telescoping of time and eternity, of the universal and the personal, which is common to all ages…and what is most particular and most immediate to our own time and place. Christ in his infinite greatness embraces all things, the divine and the human, the spiritual and the material, the old and the new, the great and the small, and in the liturgy he makes Himself all things to all men and becomes all in all. The works which Christ accomplished in time remain in eternity, treasured in the Sacred Heart from which they come forth, and the liturgical mysteries make these works present to us each time they are celebrated. Not only that, the liturgy incorporates us in His mysteries and renews their effect in time and in space. By the liturgy, while remaining in time, we enter into the great celebration that takes place before the throne of the Lamb in heaven, in eternity.

THOMAS MERTON, *SEASONS OF CELEBRATION*, 56–57

CHRIST THE ETERNAL ROCK

I do not want you to be unaware, brothers and sisters, that our ancestors were all under the cloud, and all passed through the sea, and all were baptized into Moses in the cloud and in the sea, and all ate the same spiritual food, and all drank the same spiritual drink. For they drank from the spiritual rock that followed them, and the rock was Christ. Nevertheless, God was not pleased with most of them, and they were struck down in the wilderness.

Now these things occurred as examples for us, so that we might not desire evil as they did. Do not become idolaters as some of them did....We must not indulge in sexual immorality as some of them did, and twenty-three thousand fell in a single day. We must not put Christ to the test, as some of them did, and were destroyed by serpents. And do not complain as some of them did, and were destroyed by the destroyer....So if you think you are standing, watch out that you do not fall. No testing has overtaken you that is not common to everyone. God is faithful, and he will not let you be tested beyond your strength, but with the testing he will also provide the way out so that you may be able to endure it.

1 CORINTHIANS 10:1–6, 8–10, 12–13

PRAYER

As it was for the Israelites wandering in the desert, it is for us today as we search for spiritual sustenance. You, O Christ, are our rock and spiritual nourishment in the Eucharist of your compassion for us. Relying on you, we pray for strength in times of temptation.

LENTEN JOURNAL

Consider how your intentions and actions have an effect in "eternity." How you influence family, friends, and others and how you pass on the good influence you received from others.

Monday in the Third Week of Lent

BECOMING A PERSON, ANSWERING CHRIST'S CALL

"What shall a man give in exchange for his soul?" That sentence is at the very heart of Christian personalism. Our soul is irreplaceable, it can be exchanged for *nothing* in heaven or on earth, but until we have heard Christ speak, until we have received His call from the midst of the Christian assembly (every vocation to the faith comes at least implicitly through the Church) and until we have given to Him that secret and unique answer which no one can pronounce in our place, until we have thus found ourselves in Him, we cannot fully realize what it means to be a "person" in the deepest sense of the word.

THOMAS MERTON, *SEASONS OF CELEBRATION*, 24

THE SPIRIT OF THE LORD IS UPON ME

When he came to Nazareth, where he had been brought up, he went to the synagogue on the sabbath day, as was his custom. He stood up to read, and the scroll of the prophet Isaiah was given to him. He unrolled the scroll and found the place where it was written:
"The Spirit of the Lord is upon me,
because he has anointed me
to bring good news to the poor.
He has sent me to proclaim release to the captives
and recovery of sight to the blind,
to let the oppressed go free,
to proclaim the year of the Lord's favor."
And he rolled up the scroll, gave it back to the attendant, and sat down. The eyes of all in the synagogue were fixed on him. Then he began to say to them, "Today this scripture has been fulfilled in your hearing." All spoke well of him and were amazed at the gracious words that came from his mouth. They said, "Is not this Joseph's son?"

LUKE 4:16–22

PRAYER

The heart of my vocation in becoming a person is hearing your word proclaimed in the assembly and my response to it. To find my own way to follow your gospel is to find my inmost identity as a person. Come, Holy Spirit, enkindle my mind to hear and strengthen my limbs to do what Jesus tells me. Encourage me to become who I already am.

LENTEN JOURNAL

What is your "Christian" vocation? How did you discover it?

DAY 21

Tuesday in the Third Week of Lent

BECOMING A MATURE CHRISTIAN

We must be able to put aside the "economic" concern with our superficial selves, and emerge into the open light of the Christian *polis* where each one lives not for himself but for others, taking upon himself the responsibility for the whole. Of course no one assumes this responsibility merely in obedience to arbitrary whim or to the delusion that he is of himself capable of taking the troubles of the whole Assembly on his own shoulders. But he emerges "in Christ" to share the labor and worship of the whole Christ, and in order to do this he must *sacrifice* his own superficial and private self. The paradoxical fruit of this sacrifice of his trivial and "selfish" (or simply immature) self is that he is then enabled to discover his deep self, in Christ.

THOMAS MERTON, *SEASONS OF CELEBRATION,* 25

DOING GOD'S WORD

"Not everyone who says to me, 'Lord, Lord,' will enter the kingdom of heaven, but only one who does the will of my Father in heaven. On that day many will say to me, 'Lord, Lord, did we not prophesy in your name, and cast out demons in your name, and do many deeds of power in your name?' Then I will declare to them, 'I never knew you; go away from me, you evildoers.'

"Everyone then who hears these words of mine and acts on them will be like a wise man who built his house on rock. The rain fell, the floods came, and the winds blew and beat on that house, but it did not fall, because it had been founded on rock. And everyone who hears these words of mine and does not act on them will be like a foolish man who built his house on sand. The rain fell, and the floods came, and the winds blew and beat against that house, and it fell—and great was its fall!"

MATTHEW 7:21–27

PRAYER

Give me the grace, Lord, to transcend my limited and private self so that I might become a Christian adult responsible for those you have given me in Christ. You have called me into the politics that struggles for a just, equitable for all, society. Let me take my place among those who care for and do justice for the poor, the disenfranchised, and all those left behind by a society that worships idols and not the Father of All and for All.

LENTEN JOURNAL

Are you "mature in Christ"? Have you taken a responsible place in your faith community?

Wednesday in the Third Week of Lent

UNION WITH CHRIST, UNION WITH THE CHURCH

*T*he liturgy is, as the Fathers taught, a work of the *active* life. It prepares us for contemplation, which is the final perfection of Christian personalism, since it is the intimate realization of one's perfect union with Christ "in one Spirit." The highest paradox of Christian personalism is for an individual to be "found in Christ Jesus" and thus "lost" to all that can be regarded, in a mundane way, as his "self." This means to be at the same time one's self and Christ. But this is not to be ascribed solely to personal initiative, "private prayer" or individual effort. Contemplation is a gift of God, given in and through His Church, and through the prayer of the Church. St. Anthony was led into the desert not by a private voice but by the word of God, proclaimed in the Church of his Egyptian village in the chanting of the Gospel in Coptic—a classical example of liturgy opening the way to a life of contemplation! But the liturgy cannot fulfill this function if we misunderstand or underestimate the essentially spiritual value of Christian public prayer. If we cling to immature and limited notions of "privacy," we will never be able to free ourselves from the bonds of individualism. We will never realize how the Church delivers us from ourselves by public worship, the very public character of which tends to hide us "in the secret of God's face."

THOMAS MERTON, SEASONS OF CELEBRATION, 26–27

HEARING GOD'S WORD IN COMMUNITY

So now, Israel, give heed to the statutes and ordinances that I am teaching you to observe, so that you may live to enter and occupy the land that the LORD, the God of your ancestors, is giving you....

See, just as the LORD my God has charged me, I now teach you statutes and ordinances for you to observe in the land that you are about to enter and occupy. You must observe them diligently, for this will show your wisdom and discernment to the peoples, who, when they hear all these statutes, will say, "Surely this great nation is a wise and discerning people!" For what other great nation has a god so near to it as the LORD our God is whenever we call to him? And what other great nation has statutes and ordinances as just as this entire law that I am setting before you today?

But take care and watch yourselves closely, so as neither to forget the things that your eyes have seen nor to let them slip from your mind all the days of your life; make them known to your children and your children's children.

DEUTERONOMY 4:1, 5–9

PRAYER

The "word" that Saint Anthony, the hermit, heard in the liturgy that changed his life was your command: "If you would be my disciple, give up everything you have and come follow me." Lord Jesus, give me a "word" for my salvation. Celebrating Eucharist, all of us listening together for a "word," let me hear what you demand of me at this moment in my life, at this stage of my journey toward maturity in Christ. Next Sunday, and every Sunday, keep me attentive to your "word" for me.

LENTEN JOURNAL

Since Lent began, what "words" have you heard for your salvation?

DAY 23

Thursday in the Third Week of Lent

CHRIST HAS REDEEMED TIME

The Liturgy accepts our common, everyday experience of time: sunrise, noonday, sunset; spring, summer, autumn, winter. There is no reason for the Church in her prayer to do anything else "with time," for the obvious reason that the Church has no quarrel with time. The Church is not fighting against time. The Christian does not, or at any rate need not, consider time an enemy. Time is not doing the Christian any harm, time is not standing between the Christian and anything he desires. Time is not robbing the Christian of anything he treasures.

Fundamentally the Christian is at peace with time because he is at peace with God. He need no longer be fearful and distrustful of time, because he understands that time is not being used by a hostile "fate" to determine his life in some sense which he himself can never know, and for which he cannot adequately be prepared. Time has now come to terms with man's freedom.

When man is not free from sin, then time is his enemy because every moment is a threat of destruction: every moment may be the one in which the unreality which man has chosen, by sinning, is brought face to face with cataclysmic reproof and is shown to be the fruit of servility, the abnegation of freedom, the surrender to determination by forces lower than man.

THOMAS MERTON, *SEASONS OF CELEBRATION*, 45–46

THEREFORE, DO NOT WORRY

"Therefore I tell you, do not worry about your life, what you will eat or what you will drink, or about your body, what you will wear. Is not life more than food, and the body more than clothing? Look at the birds of the air; they neither sow nor reap nor gather into barns, and yet your heavenly Father feeds them. Are you not of more value than they? And can any of you by worrying add a single hour to your span of life? And why do you worry about clothing? Consider the lilies of the field, how they grow; they neither toil nor spin, yet I tell you, even Solomon in all his glory was not clothed like one of these. But if God so clothes the grass of the field, which is alive today and tomorrow is thrown into the oven, will he not much more clothe you—you of little faith? Therefore do not worry, saying, 'What will we eat?' or 'What will we drink?' or 'What will we wear?' For it is the Gentiles who strive for all these things; and indeed your heavenly Father knows that you need all these things. But strive first for the kingdom of God and his righteousness, and all these things will be given to you as well.

"So do not worry about tomorrow, for tomorrow will bring worries of its own. Today's trouble is enough for today."

MATTHEW 6:25–34

PRAYER

May each day I live be the "acceptable" time for me, time to receive a day's blessings and the challenges of hearing and doing your word. Time is on my side, Lord, because of your fulfillment of the Father's word in our time.

LENTEN JOURNAL

What are you doing with "time" these days? Fighting it? Losing it? Saving it? Spending it? Enjoying it?

DAY 24

Friday in the Third Week of Lent

CHRISTIAN FREEDOM OF CHOICE

*B*ut when man recovers, in Christ, the freedom of the Sons of God, he lives in time without *predetermination*, because grace will always protect his freedom against the tyranny of evil. The Christian then knows that time does not murmur an implicit threat of enslavement and final destruction. Time on the contrary gives scope for his freedom and his life. Time gives free play to gratitude and to that sacrifice of praise which is the full expression of the Christian's sonship in the Spirit. In other words time does not *limit* freedom, but gives it scope for its exercise and choice. Time for the Christian is then the sphere of his spontaneity, a sacramental gift in which he can allow his freedom to deploy itself in joy, in the creative virtuosity of choice that is always blessed with the full consciousness that God wants His sons and daughter to be free.

THOMAS MERTON, *SEASONS OF CELEBRATION*, 46

The Freedom to Return to the Lord

Return, O Israel, to the LORD your God,
for you have stumbled because of your iniquity.
Take words with you
and return to the LORD;
say to him,
"Take away all guilt;
accept that which is good,
and we will offer the fruit of our lips.
Assyria shall not save us;
we will not ride upon horses;
we will say no more, 'Our God,'
to the work of our hands.
In you the orphan finds mercy."

I will heal their disloyalty;
I will love them freely,
for my anger has turned from them.

HOSEA 14:1–4

Prayer

I offer you, Lord, my time, this gift of the fullness of life in time that I now experience in being united to you. Help me to redeem time for others. Help me to unburden their load of stress. By your grace let me be an instrument of your call to freedom and creativity in the lives of all whom you redeem. Let them hear your call to the only liberty that matters: to choose to follow you.

Lenten Journal

What would you like to be free from? What would you do if you were? What's preventing you from doing what you want to be free to do?

DAY 25

Saturday in the Third Week of Lent

TIME IS THE MEDIUM OF OUR SALVATION

*T*he redemption is...an ever present reality, living and efficacious, penetrating the inmost depths of our being by the work of salvation and the mystery of faith. The redemption is Christ Himself, "who of God is made to us wisdom and justice and sanctification and redemption" (1 Corinthians 1:30) living and sharing His divine life with His elect. To be redeemed is not merely to be absolved of guilt before God, it is also to live in Christ, to be born again of water and the Holy Spirit, to be in Him a new creature, to live in the Spirit.

To say that the redemption is an ever present spiritual reality is to say that Christ has laid hold upon time and sanctified it, giving it a sacramental character, making it an efficacious sign of our union with God in Him. So "time" is a medium which makes the fact of the redemption present to all men.

THOMAS MERTON, *SEASONS OF CELEBRATION*, 48–49

RENEWAL IN TIME: BEING BORN AGAIN

Purge me with hyssop, and I shall be clean;
   wash me, and I shall be whiter than snow.
Let me hear joy and gladness;
   let the bones that you have crushed rejoice.
Hide your face from my sins,
   and blot out all my iniquities.
Create in me a clean heart, O God,
   and put a new and right spirit within me.
Do not cast me away from your presence,
   and do not take your holy spirit from me.
Restore to me the joy of your salvation,
   and sustain in me a willing spirit.
Then I will teach transgressors your ways,
   and sinners will return to you.
Deliver me from bloodshed, O God,
   O God of my salvation,
   and my tongue will sing aloud of your deliverance.
O Lord, open my lips,
   and my mouth will declare your praise.

PSALM 51:7–15

PRAYER

Every day of my life is an opportunity to renew my joy in your salvific work in me and the community of all human beings with whom I am now sharing time. Come, Holy Spirit, enkindle within us again today the fire of your love.

LENTEN JOURNAL

With whom do you most "share time"? With whom should you be sharing more time?

DAY 26

Fourth Sunday of Lent

EVERY DAY IS THE "DAY OF THE LORD"

*C*hrist has given a special meaning and power to the cycle of the seasons, which of themselves are "good" and by their very nature have a capacity to signify our life in God: for the seasons express the rhythm of natural life. They are the systole and diastole of the natural life of our globe. Jesus has made this ebb and flow of light and darkness, activity and rest, birth and death, the sign of a higher life, a life which we live in Him, a life which knows no decline, and a day which does not fall into darkness. It is the "day of the Lord" which dawns for us anew each morning, the day of Easter, the "eighth day," the *Pascha Domini*, the day of eternity, shining upon us in time.

THOMAS MERTON, *SEASONS OF CELEBRATION*, 49

Every Day I Rise Again Toward the Father

Then Jesus said, "There was a man who had two sons. The younger of them said to his father, 'Father, give me the share of the property that will belong to me.' So he divided his property between them. A few days later the younger son gathered all he had and traveled to a distant country, and there he squandered his property in dissolute living. When he had spent everything, a severe famine took place throughout that country, and he began to be in need. So he went and hired himself out to one of the citizens of that country, who sent him to his fields to feed the pigs. He would gladly have filled himself with the pods that the pigs were eating; and no one gave him anything. But when he came to himself he said, 'How many of my father's hired hands have bread enough and to spare, but here I am dying of hunger! I will get up and go to my father, and I will say to him, "Father, I have sinned against heaven and before you; I am no longer worthy to be called your son; treat me like one of your hired hands."' So he set off and went to his father."

LUKE 15:11–20A

Prayer

Each day that I repent of my sins is my personal Easter. Each day I remember to turn home toward you is my participation in the resurrection of your Son. Though I stumble, let me always get up again, trusting always in your open, welcoming arms.

Lenten Journal

In your life "with and in Christ," what is the most significant part of the day for you? What season of the year is most significant?

DAY 27

Monday in the Fourth Week of Lent

COMMUNION IN FORGIVENESS

*I*f the unity of Christians in One Body makes the Church a sign of God in the world, and if men tend unfortunately to conflict and division by reason of their weakness, selfishness and sin, then the will to reconciliation and pardon is necessary if the Church is to make God visible in the world. Nor can this pardon, this communion in forgiveness, remain interior and invisible. It must be clearly manifest. So the mystery of the Church demands that Christians love one another in a visible and concrete way....Christ will be not be visible to the world in His Church except in proportion as Christians seek peace and unity with one another and with all men. But since conflict is inevitable, unity cannot be maintained except in great difficulty, with constantly renewed sacrifice, with lucid honesty, openness, humility, the readiness to ask forgiveness and to forgive.

THOMAS MERTON, *SEASONS OF CELEBRATION*, 216–217

THE SIN OF JUDGING

"Do not judge, and you will not be judged; do not condemn, and you will not be condemned. Forgive, and you will be forgiven; give, and it will be given to you. A good measure, pressed down, shaken together, running over, will be put into your lap; for the measure you give will be the measure you get back."

He also told them a parable: "Can a blind person guide a blind person? Will not both fall into a pit? A disciple is not above the teacher, but everyone who is fully qualified will be like the teacher. Why do you see the speck in your neighbor's eye, but do not notice the log in your own eye? Or how can you say to your neighbor, 'Friend, let me take out the speck in your eye,' when you yourself do not see the log in your own eye? You hypocrite, first take the log out of your own eye, and then you will see clearly to take the speck out of your neighbor's eye."

LUKE 6:37–42

PRAYER

Not a day goes by that I do not find myself judging and condemning the sins and failures of others. With the slightest examination of my conscience, my lack of compassion is obvious to me. Soften my judging heart, Lord. Let me see myself for who I truly am, a sinner among sinners. Quiet my judging heart.

LENTEN JOURNAL

If Lent is the Church's call to forgive and to be forgiven, how are you answering it?

Tuesday in the Fourth Week of Lent

FORGIVENESS IS THE EPIPHANY OF GOD'S LOVE

*I*nsofar as the Church is a community of pardon it is an epiphany of the Divine Love, Agape....This love is the key to everything, but it cannot be known, discovered or understood by rational investigation alone. It must be revealed to men in a free gift of God. It is revealed to them in the gift of love. God has willed that men should know Him not in esoteric secrets and strange philosophies, but in the announcement of the Gospel message which is the message of His love. "This is my commandment, that you love one another as I have loved you" (John 15:12). "You have not chosen me but I have chosen you, and have appointed you that you should go and bear fruit....These things I command you that you may love one another" (John 15:16–17). The love of Christians, commanded by God and carried out by them, makes them "God's workmanship" (Ephesians 2:10, *NIV*).

THOMAS MERTON, *SEASONS OF CELEBRATION*, 217

BEING IN THE LIGHT

Beloved, I am writing you no new commandment, but an old commandment that you have had from the beginning; the old commandment is the word that you have heard. Yet I am writing you a new commandment that is true in him and in you, because the darkness is passing away and the true light is already shining. Whoever says, "I am in the light," while hating a brother or sister, is still in the darkness. Whoever loves a brother or sister lives in the light, and in such a person there is no cause for stumbling. But whoever hates another believer is in the darkness, walks in the darkness, and does not know the way to go, because the darkness has brought on blindness.

1 JOHN 2:7–11

PRAYER

Overturn all hate in me and the spirit of divisiveness. Let no one be shut out from my prayers. Teach me to forgive as I wish to be forgiven. I need your love and grace to live as you teach me to live.

LENTEN JOURNAL

How difficult is it for you to forgive and pardon others and yourself? Is there still someone you haven't forgiven?

DAY 29

Wednesday in the Fourth Week of Lent

THE MYSTERY OF OUR COMMUNION IN LOVE

The word of the Gospel is understood only when it is obeyed. It is known to those who strive to practice it. Yet it is also more than a moral doctrine that can be preached by example. To receive the word of the Gospel, the Kerygma of God's love for man in Christ, of God's gift of Himself to man in Christ, is to enter into the living and active communion of love which has become the center of salvation history. This communion itself is a profound religious mystery, for it is participation not only in a natural love of man for his brother and sister, but in the love of God for sinful man as revealed in the mystery of the Cross and Resurrection of Jesus Christ.

To enter fully into this mystery one must receive the Holy Spirit, who is the Love of God (1 Corinthians 2:10–12).

THOMAS MERTON, *SEASONS OF CELEBRATION*, 217–218

THE HOLY SPIRIT, SOURCE OF OUR UNITY IN CHRIST

Yet among the mature we do speak wisdom, though it is not a wisdom of this age or of the rulers of this age, who are doomed to perish. But we speak God's wisdom, secret and hidden, which God decreed before the ages for our glory. None of the rulers of this age understood this; for if they had, they would not have crucified the Lord of glory. But, as it is written,

"What no eye has seen, nor ear heard,
nor the human heart conceived,
what God has prepared for those who love him"—
these things God has revealed to us through the Spirit; for the Spirit searches everything, even the depths of God.... And we speak of these things in words not taught by human wisdom but taught by the Spirit, interpreting spiritual things to those who are spiritual.

Those who are unspiritual do not receive the gifts of God's Spirit, for they are foolishness to them, and they are unable to understand them because they are spiritually discerned. Those who are spiritual discern all things, and they are themselves subject to no one else's scrutiny.

"For who has known the mind of the Lord
so as to instruct him?"
But we have the mind of Christ.

1 CORINTHIANS 2:6–10, 13–16

PRAYER

Spirit of love and communion, give me grace to understand the mind of Christ. Let me do his will by obedience to the revelation of the Father's will that all of us be "one body." I cannot understand the depths of this mystery. Give me the grace to love it.

LENTEN JOURNAL

Consider your relationship to the Holy Spirit.

DAY 30

Thursday in the Fourth Week of Lent

RECONCILIATION IN CHRIST

*A*s Christ passed through death to life in the Spirit (see 1 Peter 3:18) so the Christian follows Christ on His Paschal Mystery through death to life. Sin is pardoned, and man is redeemed not by the destruction and punishment of man's freedom, but by its purification.

It is precisely in his freedom that man accepts the redemptive power of the Cross. It is man's freedom that is nailed to the Cross with Christ and rises to a new life in the Christian agape. That is to say that each individual renounces what is purely selfish and confesses his wrong, in order to find himself on the new spiritual level of reconciliation in Christ. But no one sincerely confesses his own sin without at the same time pardoning his brother (see Matthew 18:23–35). Forgiveness of sins is proclaimed to the world in Christ, and is granted to each one whom, in the act of seeking pardon, himself pardons others and makes himself an instrument of the divine mercy. Sin cannot be pardoned and healed without love, because all sin is, at its root, a refusal of love. No matter how great our sin may be, it is forgiven when we consent to love (see Luke 7:47). The Sacrament of penance is instituted as the visible sign of this reconciliation and hence it is required that we receive it before we return from mortal sin to Eucharistic Communion, the sign of our life in Christ's love.

THOMAS MERTON, *SEASONS OF CELEBRATION,* 218–219

RECONCILIATION WITH OUR NEIGHBORS

"You have heard that it was said to those of ancient times, 'You shall not murder'; and 'whoever murders shall be liable to judgment.' But I say to you that if you are angry with a brother or sister, you will be liable to judgment; and if you insult a brother or sister, you will be liable to the council; and if you say, 'You fool,' you will be liable to the hell of fire. So when you are offering your gift at the altar, if you remember that your brother or sister has something against you, leave your gift there before the altar and go; first be reconciled to your brother or sister, and then come and offer your gift."

MATTHEW 5:21–24

PRAYER

Reconcile my heart. Give me the grace to ask forgiveness of those I have offended and to forgive those who have offended me. If I cannot at least pray for everyone, I cannot be your disciple. What you ask of me, Lord, is a life's work of reconciliation. Let me at least begin to labor at forgiveness.

LENTEN JOURNAL

How is forgiveness and reconciliation linked to freedom in my life?

DAY 31

Friday in the Fourth Week of Lent

RECONCILIATION IN THE SPIRIT OF LOVE

The Gospel is then a message of reconciliation in the Spirit of Love. Those who receive the Holy Spirit are reconciled to God and to one another in love. The supreme purpose of all life is then to receive the Holy Spirit, to live by the Spirit of Christ, to have Him dwelling and acting in our hearts (John 7:37–39). And it is for this that the Spirit awakens in our hearts faith in Christ and draws us to the Church, which is the Living Body of Christ. When we live as members of Christ, we receive the Holy Spirit. The sacraments of the Church give us participation in the life of the Spirit. Faith awakens that life in our hearts. Love is the guarantee that the life of the Spirit is growing in us. He who confesses Christ and loves his brother and sister, who forgets himself in order to help his brother and sister and who devotes his life to the truth of the Gospel, lives and grows in the Spirit.

THOMAS MERTON, *SEASONS OF CELEBRATION*, 219–220

A River of Living Water

Jesus then said, "I will be with you a little while longer, and then I am going to him who sent me. You will search for me, but you will not find me; and where I am, you cannot come." The Jews said to one another, "Where does this man intend to go that we will not find him? Does he intend to go to the Dispersion among the Greeks and teach the Greeks? What does he mean by saying, 'You will search for me and you will not find me' and 'Where I am, you cannot come'?"

On the last day of the festival, the great day, while Jesus was standing there, he cried out, "Let anyone who is thirsty come to me, and let the one who believes in me drink. As the scripture has said, 'Out of the believer's heart shall flow rivers of living water.'" Now he said this about the Spirit, which believers in him were to receive; for as yet there was no Spirit, because Jesus was not yet glorified.

JOHN 7:33–39

Prayer

How many times in my life have I been thirsty and someone gave me water? How many times have I been in pain and someone comforted me? How many times have I been lost and someone showed me another road? How many times have I received you, Holy Spirit, source of my life and pledge of my resurrection in Christ, and did not know it?

Lenten Journal

Who in your life has been a Spirit-bearer to you?

DAY 32

Saturday in the Fourth Week of Lent

SEEKING GOD IN COMMUNITY

We must in all things seek God. But we do not seek Him the way we seek a lost object, a "thing." He is present to us in our heart, in our personal subjectivity, and to seek Him is to recognize this fact. Yet we cannot be aware of it as a reality unless He reveals His presence to us. He does not reveal Himself simply in our own heart. He reveals Himself to us in the Church, in the community of believers, in the *koinonia* of those who trust Him and love Him.

Seeking God is not just an operation of the intellect, or even a contemplative illumination of the mind. We seek God by striving to surrender ourselves to Him whom we do not see, but Who is in all things and through all things and above all things.

THOMAS MERTON, *SEASONS OF CELEBRATION*, 223–224

The Service of Love

After he had washed their feet, had put on his robe, and had returned to the table, he said to them, "Do you know what I have done to you? You call me Teacher and Lord—and you are right, for that is what I am. So if I, your Lord and Teacher, have washed your feet, you also ought to wash one another's feet. For I have set you an example, that you also should do as I have done to you. Very truly, I tell you, servants are not greater than their master, nor are messengers greater than the one who sent them. If you know these things, you are blessed if you do them."

JOHN 13:12–17

Prayer

I cannot be saved without everyone else being saved with me. I cannot be saved if I am not saved by others who love God and are struggling to follow Christ. I am never alone with God. O most holy Trinity, undivided unity, God immortal community, be adored.

Lenten Journal

Who is "the Church" for you? In what ways do you experience God's revelation to you?

░░░ DAY 33 ░░░░░░░░░░░░░░░░░░░░░░░░░░░░░░░░░░░░░

Fifth Sunday of Lent

THE KISS OF PEACE

The highest adoration we offer to God, "in spirit and in truth," is in this sharing of the breath of the Divine Spirit with one another in pardon and in love. That is why we are told to forgive one another before we go to offer sacrifice. That is why we exchange the kiss of peace before Communion. The kiss of peace is in some way part of our Eucharistic communion: it symbolizes the spiritual sharing of the Holy Spirit. With a holy kiss we give the Holy Spirit to one another, as if the flame of one candle were transferred to enlighten another.

THOMAS MERTON, *SEASONS OF CELEBRATION*, 227

Unless a Grain of Wheat Dies

"Very truly, I tell you, unless a grain of wheat falls into the earth and dies, it remains just a single grain; but if it dies, it bears much fruit. Those who love their life lose it, and those who hate their life in this world will keep it for eternal life. Whoever serves me must follow me, and where I am, there will my servant be also. Whoever serves me, the Father will honor.

"Now my soul is troubled. And what should I say—'Father, save me from this hour'? No, it is for this reason that I have come to this hour. Father, glorify your name." Then a voice came from heaven, "I have glorified it, and I will glorify it again." The crowd standing there heard it and said that it was thunder. Others said, "An angel has spoken to him." Jesus answered, "This voice has come for your sake, not for mine. Now is the judgment of this world; now the ruler of this world will be driven out. And I, when I am lifted up from the earth, will draw all people to myself."

John 12:24–32

Prayer

Let me die to myself and live for those gathered in your name. Let me humble myself before the breadth and height and depth of your love for all beings. Let me see your face in every face I see. With everyone else, I journey toward you.

Lenten Journal

Consider how becoming God's servant is an act of dying to yourself that bears much fruit.

DAY 34

Monday in the Fifth Week of Lent

WE ARE A COMMUNITY OF PARDON

We are a community of pardon, not a community of judgment. We are told not to judge one another and we must not. We must not judge in such a way as to reject and condemn. That is to say we not refuse to accept the genuine good will of our brother and sister; we not reject their sincere and open offers of reconciliation, their true friendship. Even our enemy must not be judged, but his need for forgiveness must be recognized. We must not judge, that is to say we must always be ready to take the first step in offering reconciliation and pardon. We must not let our evaluations of a man's acts stand in the way of the Holy Spirit, who draws us to unity with the "other" in spite of his actions which make him different from ourselves, perhaps opposed to us.

We have a duty to pardon, because it is through us that God wishes to pardon all sinners.

THOMAS MERTON, *SEASONS OF CELEBRATION*, 228–229

LOVING ALL, SERVING ALL

"You have heard that it was said, 'An eye for an eye and a tooth for a tooth.' But I say to you, Do not resist an evildoer. But if anyone strikes you on the right cheek, turn the other also; and if anyone wants to sue you and take your coat, give your cloak as well; and if anyone forces you to go one mile, go also the second mile. Give to everyone who begs from you, and do not refuse anyone who wants to borrow from you."

MATTHEW 5:38–42

PRAYER

The cost of following your way is everything, isn't it? No cheap grace, though I would love to have found it. Your cross that brings eternal life is a stake in the heart of everything my sinful self holds dear. You are uncompromising in your commandment to be in communion with everyone. Help me, without your aid I cannot possibly swim in the open sea of your love.

LENTEN JOURNAL

In what ways is Christ's command that we "pardon one another" a stumbling block for you? Is it impossible for you to do what Christ demands to become his disciple?

DAY 35

Tuesday in the Fifth Week of Lent

NO MAN IS AN ISLAND

In building a community of pardon that is the temple of God, we have to recognize that no one of us is complete, self-sufficient, perfectly holy in himself. No one can rest in his own individual virtues and interior life. No man lives for himself alone. To live for oneself alone is to die. We grow and flourish in our own lives insofar as we live for others and through others. What we ourselves lack, God has given them. They must complete us where we are deficient. Hence we must always remain open to one another so that we can always share with each other.

The greatest of gifts then is this openness, this love, this readiness to accept and to pardon and to share with others, in the Spirit of Christ. If we are open we will not only offer pardon, but will not disdain to seek it and recognize our own desperate need of it.

THOMAS MERTON, *SEASONS OF CELEBRATION*, 229

LOVING ONE ANOTHER IN DEED AND IN TRUTH

For this is the message you have heard from the beginning, that we should love one another. We must not be like Cain who was from the evil one and murdered his brother. And why did he murder him? Because his own deeds were evil and his brother's righteous. Do not be astonished, brothers and sisters, that the world hates you. We know that we have passed from death to life because we love one another. Whoever does not love abides in death. All who hate a brother or sister are murderers, and you know that murderers do not have eternal life abiding in them. We know love by this, that he laid down his life for us—and we ought to lay down our lives for one another. How does God's love abide in anyone who has the world's goods and sees a brother or sister in need and yet refuses help?

Little children, let us love, not in word or speech, but in truth and action.

1 JOHN 3:11–18

PRAYER

Let me bring to the table of Christ's Eucharist my need for forgiveness. Let me acknowledge with my fellow Christians our need for forgiveness. Then, by your grace, Spirit of our redemption, let me forgive.

LENTEN JOURNAL

With whom in your life do you sense that you are "in communion"?

DAY 36

Wednesday in the Fifth Week of Lent

A LOVE WITHOUT WALLS

*I*f a person has to be pleasing to me, comforting, reassuring, before I can love him, then I cannot truly love him. Not that love cannot console or reassure! But if I demand *first* to be reassured, I will never dare to begin loving. If a person has to be a Jew or a Christian before I can love him, then I cannot love him. If he has to be black or white before I can love him, then I cannot love him. If he has to belong to my political party or social group before I can love him, then I cannot love him. If he has to wear my kind of uniform, then my love is no longer love because it is not free: it is dictated by something outside itself. It is dominated by an appetite other than love. I love not the person but his classification, and in that I love him not as person but as a thing. I love his label which confirms me in my attachment to my own label. But in that case I do not even love myself. I value myself not for what I am, but for my label, my classification. In this way I remain at the mercy of forces outside myself, and those who seem to me to be neighbors are indeed strangers for I am first of all a stranger to myself.

THOMAS MERTON, *SEASONS OF CELEBRATION*, 174

GOD IS LOVE

Beloved, let us love one another, because love is from God; everyone who loves is born of God and knows God. Whoever does not love does not know God, for God is love. God's love was revealed among us in this way: God sent his only Son into the world so that we might live through him. In this is love, not that we loved God but that he loved us and sent his Son to be the atoning sacrifice for our sins. Beloved, since God loved us so much, we also ought to love one another. No one has ever seen God; if we love one another, God lives in us, and his love is perfected in us.

1 JOHN 4:7–12

PRAYER

Holy Spirit God, save us from our enclosed communities of faith. Save us from our churches of meanness. Save us from our blindness to your great commandment that we love one another as we should love you: with all our mind, all our heart, and all our strength.

LENTEN JOURNAL

In what ways can you make your faith community more loving of everyone?

DAY 37

Thursday in the Fifth Week of Lent

THE REALITY OF GOD'S MERCY

*T*he parable of the Good Samaritan is a revelation of God in a word that has great importance through all the Scriptures from beginning to the end. It is a revelation of what the prophet Hosea says, speaking for the invisible God, "I will have *mercy* and not sacrifices." What is this *mercy* which we find spoken everywhere in the Scriptures, and especially in the Psalms? The Vulgate rings with *misericordia* as though with a deep church bell. Mercy is the "burden" or the "bourdon," it is the brass bell and undersong of the whole Bible. But the Hebrew word—*chesed*—which we render as mercy, misericordia, says more still than mercy.

Chesed (mercy) is also fidelity, it is also strength. It is the faithful, the indefectible mercy of God. It is ultimate and unfailing because it is the power that binds one person to another, in a covenant of wills. It is the power that binds us to God because He has promised us mercy and will never fail in His promise.

For He cannot fail. It is the power and the mercy which are most characteristic of Him, which come nearer to the mystery into which we enter when all concepts darken and evade us.

THOMAS MERTON, *SEASONS OF CELEBRATION*, 175

GOD HAS LOVED US FROM OUR BEGINNING

Love has been perfected among us in this: that we may have boldness on the day of judgment, because as he is, so are we in this world. There is no fear in love, but perfect love casts out fear; for fear has to do with punishment, and whoever fears has not reached perfection in love. We love because he first loved us. Those who say, "I love God," and hate their brothers or sisters, are liars; for those who do not love a brother or sister whom they have seen, cannot love God whom they have not seen. The commandment we have from him is this: those who love God must love their brothers and sisters also.

1 JOHN 4:17–21

PRAYER

You loved me before I knew I was lovable. The loving kindness you have shown me through the chorus of persons in my life who have had mercy on me fills me with gratitude. You love me through them. To them and you I return my thanks and offer you this day's hymn of praise.

LENTEN JOURNAL

Who has been "faithful" to you in your life? Who has most treated you with an abiding, "loving kindness"?

Friday in the Fifth Week of Lent

SACRAMENTS OF MERCY

*T*he *chesed* of God is a gratuitous mercy that considers no fitness, no worthiness and no return. It is the way the Lord looks upon the guilty and with His look makes them at once innocent. This look seems to some to be anger because they fly from it. But if they face it, they see that it is love and that they are innocent. (Their flight and their confusion of their own fear make them guilty in their own eyes.) The *chesed* of God is truth. It is infallible strength. It is the love by which He seeks and chooses his chosen, and binds them to Himself. It is the love by which He is married to mankind, so that, if humanity is faithless to Him, it must still always have fidelity to which to return: that is His own fidelity. He has become inseparable from man in the *chesed* which we call "Incarnation," and "Cross" and "Resurrection." He has also given us His *chesed* in the Person of His Spirit. The Paraclete is the full, inexpressible mystery of *chesed*. So that in the depths of our own being there is an inexhaustible spring of mercy and love. Our own being has become love. Our own self has become God's love for us, and it is full of Christ, of *chesed*. But we must face and accept ourselves and others as chesed. We must be to ourselves and to others signs and sacraments of mercy.

THOMAS MERTON, SEASONS OF CELEBRATION, 178–179

BLESSED ARE THE MERCIFUL

Then Jesus went about all the cities and villages, teaching in their synagogues, and proclaiming the good news of the kingdom, and curing every disease and every sickness. When he saw the crowds, he had compassion for them, because they were harassed and helpless, like sheep without a shepherd. Then he said to his disciples, "The harvest is plentiful, but the laborers are few; therefore ask the Lord of the harvest to send out laborers into his harvest."

MATTHEW 9:35–38

PRAYER

O God, most merciful and compassionate, heal the wounds of your Church. Raise up men and women who will be sacraments of your mercy and compassion for all of us gathered in your name and as a sign to everyone that God is love.

LENTEN JOURNAL

Who among public figures do you regard as "sacraments of mercy" in our world?

DAY 39

Saturday in the Fifth Week of Lent

THE SAINTS ARE INSTRUMENTS OF THE DIVINE MERCY

*C*hesed, mercy and power, manifests itself visibly in the *chasid*, or the saint. Indeed the saint is one whose whole life is immersed in the *chesed* of God. The saint is the instrument of the divine mercy. Through the *chasid* the love of God reaches into the world in a visible mystery, a mystery of poverty and love, meekness and power. The *chasid* is in many respects a foolish one, who has been made comical by mercy. For the apparent tragedy of his nothingness is turned inside out with joy. In his folly the divine wisdom shines forth and his annihilation is a new creation, so that he rejoices in the incongruity of the divine mercies and is everlastingly astonished at the creative love of God. He calls upon all beings to praise this love with him, and most of them do not pay attention. Yet the sun and moon and the sea and the hills and stars join him, nevertheless, in praising *chesed*. The majority of men, perhaps, consider him crazy.

(God, too, is glad to be thought crazy in His *chasid*. For the wisdom of God is folly in the eyes of men.)

THOMAS MERTON, *SEASONS OF CELEBRATION*, 179

CHRIST THE SUFFERING SERVANT

Here is my servant, whom I uphold,
my chosen, in whom my soul delights;
I have put my spirit upon him;
he will bring forth justice to the nations.
He will not cry or lift up his voice,
or make it heard in the street;
a bruised reed he will not break,
and a dimly burning wick he will not quench;
he will faithfully bring forth justice.
He will not grow faint or be crushed
until he has established justice in the earth;
and the coastlands wait for his teaching.

ISAIAH 42:1–4

PRAYER

In communion with all the saints, I enter Holy Week to praise the great work the Father has done in you, Jesus. You responded to your mission with great courage and love. You want me to follow you and be your disciple. Send your Holy Spirit to me for my encouragement.

LENTEN JOURNAL

Who are your life's true "patron saints"?

DAY 40

Passion Sunday

WITH CHRIST IN OUR BLOODSTREAM

*T*he liturgical cycle renews our redemption in Christ, delivers us from the servitude of sin and from the corruption of a "fleshly" mode of being. The liturgical cycle shows us that though we are caught in a struggle between flesh and spirit, though we are indeed the "fighting Church"—the Church militant—yet the victory is already ours. We possess the grace of Christ, who alone can deliver us from the "body of this death." He who is in us is greater than the world. He has "overcome the world." In the cycle of the holy year, the Church rhythmically breathes the life-giving atmosphere of the Spirit, and her blood-stream is cleansed of the elements of death. She lives in Christ, and with Him praises the Father.

THOMAS MERTON, *SEASONS OF CELEBRATION*, 52–53

Blessed Is He Who Comes in God's Name

As he rode along, people kept spreading their cloaks on the road. As he was now approaching the path down from the Mount of Olives, the whole multitude of the disciples began to praise God joyfully with a loud voice for all the deeds of power that they had seen, saying,

"Blessed is the king
who comes in the name of the Lord!
Peace in heaven,
and glory in the highest heaven!"

Some of the Pharisees in the crowd said to him, "Teacher, order your disciples to stop." He answered, "I tell you, if these were silent, the stones would shout out."

As he came near and saw the city, he wept over it, saying, "If you, even you, had only recognized on this day the things that make for peace! But now they are hidden from your eyes."

LUKE 19:36–42

Prayer

Today I unite myself with every person, of every faith, who regards Jerusalem as their holy city. I consider the tears of Jesus. Wash me in your tears, Lord, as I ponder my ignorance of your peace.

Lenten Journal

Consider the rhythm of the liturgical cycle and how it can bring a life-giving cleansing to your life.

Monday of Passion Week

HOLY WEEK IS A SCHOOL OF CHRISTIAN LIVING

The mysteries of the liturgical cycle not only bring new outpourings of the salvific waters of grace: they also enlighten our minds with insights into the ways of God, ever ancient and ever new. They teach us more of Christ, they show us more of the meaning of our life in Him, they make us grow in Him, they transform us in Him. Indeed, the liturgy is the great school of Christian living and the transforming force which reshapes our souls and our characters in the likeness of Christ.

THOMAS MERTON, *SEASONS OF CELEBRATION*, 53

CHRIST IS THE RESURRECTION AND THE LIFE

When Martha heard that Jesus was coming, she went and met him, while Mary stayed at home. Martha said to Jesus, "Lord, if you had been here, my brother would not have died. But even now I know that God will give you whatever you ask of him." Jesus said to her, "Your brother will rise again." Martha said to him, "I know that he will rise again in the resurrection on the last day." Jesus said to her, "I am the resurrection and the life. Those who believe in me, even though they die, will live, and everyone who lives and believes in me will never die. Do you believe this?" She said to him, "Yes, Lord, I believe that you are the Messiah, the Son of God, the one coming into the world."

JOHN 11:20–27

PRAYER

Increase my faith in you. Increase my hope, my courage and my love. I have no where else to go. You, Lord, have the words of eternal life.

LENTEN JOURNAL

Imagine you are Lazarus risen from the dead. You are at table with Jesus and your sisters: have you anything to say?

DAY 42

Tuesday of Passion Week

THE CHRISTIAN RING

*D*om Odo Casel compared the liturgical year to a ring that the Church, the virgin bride of Christ, triumphantly displays as the sign of her union with the incarnate Word. This holy ring is the gift of Christ to His Church as a pledge of His love and of His fidelity to His promises. The "cycle" or "circle" of the liturgy, which eternally returns to its beginning, is a symbol of the unity of God who is eternally the same yet ever new.

More than that, however, the liturgical "ring" of feasts is a symbol of that first "cycle" of actions by which Christ redeemed the world—the "ring" created by His descent into time, His life, death, resurrection and ascension into heaven restoring all things, in Himself, to the Father.

THOMAS MERTON, *SEASONS OF CELEBRATION*, 54

THE LORD'S ETERNALLY NEW COMMANDMENT

When he had gone out, Jesus said, "Now the Son of Man has been glorified, and God has been glorified in him. If God has been glorified in him, God will also glorify him in himself and will glorify him at once. Little children, I am with you only a little longer. You will look for me; and as I said to the Jews so now I say to you, 'Where I am going, you cannot come.' I give you a new commandment, that you love one another. Just as I have loved you, you also should love one another. By this everyone will know that you are my disciples, if you have love for one another."

JOHN 13:31–35

PRAYER

Restore all of us more deeply to yourself in these holy days to come, Jesus, as we remember your work for the world's salvation. Redeem us in our time, Lord, while there is yet time for us to renew our discipleship and follow your way.

LENTEN JOURNAL

How are you preparing yourself to enter into the holy days ahead?

DAY 43

Wednesday of Passion Week

THE TIME TO TURN TO GOD

All the faithful should listen to the word as it is announced in the liturgy or in Bible services and respond according to their ability. In this way, for the whole Church, Lent will not be merely a season simply of a few formalized penitential practices, half-understood and undertaken without interest, but a time of *metanoia,* the turning of all mind and hearts to God in preparation for the celebration of the Paschal Mystery in which some will for the first time receive the light of Christ, others will be restored to the communion of the faithful, and all will renew their baptismal consecration of their lives to God, in Christ.

THOMAS MERTON, *SEASONS OF CELEBRATION,* 114

Opening the Ears of Our Hearts

The Lord GOD has given me
the tongue of a teacher,
that I may know how to sustain
the weary with a word.
Morning by morning he wakens—
wakens my ear
to listen as those who are taught.
The Lord GOD has opened my ear,
and I was not rebellious,
I did not turn backward.
I gave my back to those who struck me,
and my cheeks to those who pulled out the beard;
I did not hide my face
from insult and spitting.
The Lord GOD helps me;
therefore I have not been disgraced;
therefore I have set my face like flint,
and I know that I shall not be put to shame.

ISAIAH 50:4–7

Prayer

I shall listen carefully as the Church proclaims the word of your saving passion and death for the sake of all worlds, all peoples, and all time. You alone are holy, you alone are Lord, you alone, Jesus Christ, are the most high.

Lenten Journal

What word or phrase can you take with you—a mantra, like "Jesus, Son of God, have mercy on me"—as you pass over these last days toward Easter?

DAY 44

Holy Thursday

IN COMMUNION WITH CHRIST'S COMPASSION

The mystery of the Good Samaritan is this, then: the mystery of *chesed*, power and mercy. In the end, it is Christ Himself who lies wounded by the roadside. It is Christ Who comes by in the person of the Samaritan. And Christ is the bond, the compassion and understanding between them. This is how the Church is made of living stones, compacted together in mercy. Where there is on the one hand a helpless one, beaten and half dead, and on the other an outcast with no moral standing and the one leans down in pity to help the other, then there takes place a divine epiphany and awakening. There is "man," there reality is made human, and in answer to this movement of compassion, a Presence is made on the earth, and the bright cloud of the majesty of God overshadows their poverty and their love. There may be no consolation in it. There may be nothing humanly charming about it. It is not necessarily like the movies. Perhaps the encounter is outwardly sordid and unattractive. But the Presence of God is brought about on earth there, and Christ is there, and God is in communion with man.

THOMAS MERTON, *SEASONS OF CELEBRATION*, 181–182

CHRIST'S HOUR

> *The spirit of the Lord GOD is upon me,*
> *because the LORD has anointed me;*
> *he has sent me to bring good news to the oppressed,*
> *to bind up the broken-hearted,*
> *to proclaim liberty to the captives,*
> *and release to the prisoners;*
> *to proclaim the year of the LORD's favor,*
> *and the day of vengeance of our God;*
> *to comfort all who mourn;*
> *to provide for those who mourn in Zion—*
> *to give them a garland instead of ashes,*
> *the oil of gladness instead of mourning,*
> *the mantle of praise instead of a faint spirit.*
> *They will be called oaks of righteousness,*
> *the planting of the LORD, to display his glory.*

ISAIAH 61:1–3

PRAYER

I unite myself with those who gather in your name to receive the sacrament of your body and blood. You have made me one with you and one with them by the power of your Holy Spirit. Unworthy, I am called to your table and your hospitality. I shall gratefully sit and eat.

LENTEN JOURNAL

Give expression to your desire to be in "holy communion" with all your neighbors in God.

Good Friday

GOD'S UNPREDICTABLE MERCY AND WISDOM

We are bound to God in *chesed*. The power of His mercy has taken hold of us and will not let go of us: therefore we have become foolish. We can no longer love wisely. And because we have emptied ourselves in this folly which He has sent upon us, we can be moved by His unpredictable wisdom, so that we love whom we love and we help whom we help, not according to plans of our own but according to the measure laid down for us in His hidden will, which knows no measure. In this folly, which is the work of His Spirit, we must love especially those who are helpless and who can do nothing for themselves. We must also receive love from them, realizing our own helplessness, and our own inability to fend for ourselves. *Chesed* has made us as though we were outcasts and sinners. *Chesed* has numbered us among the aliens and the strangers: *chesed* has not only robbed us of our reason but declassified us along with everyone else, in the sight of

God. Thus we have no home, no family, no niche in society, and no recognizable function. Nor do we ever appear to be especially charitable, and we cannot pride ourselves on virtue. *Chesed* has apparently robbed us of all that, for he who lives by the mercy of God alone shall have nothing else to live by, only that mercy. *Plenitudo legis est charitas.* Mercy fulfills the whole law.

Thomas Merton, Seasons of Celebration, 181

The Mystery of God's Mercy and Love

Two others also, who were criminals, were led away to be put to death with him....One of the criminals who were hanged there kept deriding him and saying, "Are you not the Messiah? Save yourself and us!" But the other rebuked him, saying, "Do you not fear God, since you are under the same sentence of condemnation? And we indeed have been condemned justly, for we are getting what we deserve for our deeds, but this man has done nothing wrong." Then he said, "Jesus, remember me when you come into your kingdom." He replied, "Truly I tell you, today you will be with me in Paradise."

Luke 23:32, 39–43

Prayer

I can spend my whole life meditating on your innocence as you accepted this death as a fulfillment of the Father's creative love on behalf of all beings. Your way promises paradise to those who give up everything to love and be merciful to all beings. Help me follow you. Give me the courage to love.

Lenten Journal

Jesus is the Good Samaritan: how has he rescued you from the ditch?

DAY 46

Holy Saturday

CHRIST'S LIGHT KNOWS NO SETTING

And so, while the cycle of time is a prison without escape for the natural man, living "in the flesh," and doomed to disappear with all the rest of his world that passes away, and while time is for the man of our cities only a linear flight from God, for the believer who lives in Christ each new day renews his participation in the mystery of Christ. Each day is a new dawn of that *lumen* Christi, the light of Christ which knows no setting.

THOMAS MERTON, *SEASONS OF CELEBRATION*, 53

A Life Hidden With Christ

So if you have been raised with Christ, seek the things that are above, where Christ is, seated at the right hand of God. Set your minds on things that are above, not on things that are on earth, for you have died, and your life is hidden with Christ in God. When Christ who is your life is revealed, then you also will be revealed with him in glory.

Put to death, therefore, whatever in you is earthly: fornication, impurity, passion, evil desire, and greed (which is idolatry). On account of these the wrath of God is coming on those who are disobedient. These are the ways you also once followed, when you were living that life. But now you must get rid of all such things—anger, wrath, malice, slander, and abusive language from your mouth. Do not lie to one another, seeing that you have stripped off the old self with its practices and have clothed yourselves with the new self, which is being renewed in knowledge according to the image of its creator.

COLOSSIANS 3:1–10

PRAYER

My heart is restless. There is much about my life I do not understand. I do not know myself. I sense that if I knew myself truly, I would know you. Give me the grace to rise out of my ignorance and move through all my unknowing toward you, Jesus, calling me out of darkness and death to life. Lead me to the paradise of your mercy.

LENTEN JOURNAL

Reflect on the peace and solitude that is death and what might be the experience of being revealed with Christ in glory.

PART II

~~~~~~~~

READINGS *for* EASTER

DAY 47

Easter Sunday

THE PASSOVER OF THE LORD INTO FREEDOM

*E*aster is not a day to be compared to the Fourth of July although it is in truth the celebration of our Christian freedom....

The Easter mystery is not celebrated only at Easter but every day in the year, because the Mass is the Paschal Mystery. Passiontide, Holy Week, Easter and the "holy fifty days" of the Easter season culminating in the celebration of Pentecost, all combine to spread the Easter mystery out before us in time in all its detail: but the fullness of Good Friday, Easter and Pentecost is also compressed within the compass of every day's Mass. For each time we participate in the sacred Mysteries, the *Pascha Domini* (The Passover of the Lord), we die with Christ, rise with Him and receive from Him the Spirit of Promise who transforms us and unites us to the Father in and through the Son.

THOMAS MERTON, *SEASONS OF CELEBRATION,* 144

THE FIRSTBORN OF ALL CREATION

He is the image of the invisible God, the firstborn of all creation; for in him all things in heaven and on earth were created, things visible and invisible, whether thrones or dominions or rulers or powers—all things have been created through him and for him. He himself is before all things, and in him all things hold together. He is the head of the body, the church; he is the beginning, the firstborn from the dead, so that he might come to have first place in everything. For in him all the fullness of God was pleased to dwell, and through him God was pleased to reconcile to himself all things, whether on earth or in heaven, by making peace through the blood of his cross.

COLOSSIANS 1:15–20

PRAYER

Reconcile today, Lord Jesus, all things and me to your Father in the power of the Holy Spirit whom you have sent to renew us in freedom and joy through the mystery of your resurrection from the dead. In the words of Saint Patrick, hear my Easter prayer: "Christ, as a light, illumine and guide me. Christ, as a shield, overshadow and cover me. Christ, be over me. Christ, be under me. Christ, be beside me, on left hand and right. Christ, this day, be within and without me. Christ, the lowly and the meek. Christ, the all-powerful. Be in the heart of each to whom I speak. In the mouth of each who speaks to me, in all who draw near me, or hear me, or see me." Alleluia.

EASTER JOURNAL

How is every day of your life an experience of Easter?

Monday of Easter Week

FREE FROM THE LAW OF LENT

*L*ent has summoned us to change our hearts, to effect in ourselves the Christian *metanoia*. But at the same time Lent has reminded us perhaps all too clearly of our own powerlessness to change our lives in any way. Lent in the liturgical year plays the role of the Law, the pedagogue, who convinces us of our sin and inflicts upon us the crushing evidence of our own nothingness. Hence it disquiets and sobers us, awakening in us perhaps some sense of that existential "dread" of the creature whose freedom suspends him over an abyss which may be an infinite meaninglessness, an abounded despair. This is the fruit of that Law which judges our freedom together with its powerlessness to impose full meaning on our lives merely by conforming to a moral code.

THOMAS MERTON, *SEASONS OF CELEBRATION,* 145

CHRIST HAS FREED US FROM THE LAW OF THE FLESH

There is therefore now no condemnation for those who are in Christ Jesus. For the law of the Spirit of life in Christ Jesus has set you free from the law of sin and of death. For God has done what the law, weakened by the flesh, could not do: by sending his own Son in the likeness of sinful flesh, and to deal with sin, he condemned sin in the flesh, so that the just requirement of the law might be fulfilled in us, who walk not according to the flesh but according to the Spirit....

For all who are led by the Spirit of God are children of God. For you did not receive a spirit of slavery to fall back into fear, but you have received a spirit of adoption. When we cry, "Abba! Father!" it is that very Spirit bearing witness with our spirit that we are children of God, and if children, then heirs, heirs of God and joint heirs with Christ—if, in fact, we suffer with him so that we may also be glorified with him.

ROMANS 8:1–4, 14–17

PRAYER

Without you I can do nothing to free myself from my habitual return to fear, to lack of hope that my life has no meaning beyond this meandering passage from my birth to my death, feeling somehow guilty that I have not been true to myself, that even your witness cannot save me. Open my mind and heart this Easter to the reality that the Holy Spirit empowers me to free myself in truth by love and service for others. Set me free to love and serve.

EASTER JOURNAL

Compose a prayer to the Holy Spirit to "set you free."

⁂ DAY 49 ⁂

Tuesday of Easter Week

THE POWER OF EASTER

*B*ut now the power of Easter has burst upon us with the resurrection of Christ. Now we find in ourselves a strength which is not our own, and which is freely given to us whenever we need it, raising us above the Law, giving us a new law which is hidden in Christ: the law of His merciful love for us. Now we no longer strive to be good because we have to, because it is a duty, but because our joy is to please Him who has given all His love to us! Now our life is full of meaning.

Easter is the hour of our own deliverance—from what? Precisely from Lent and from its hard Law which accuses and judges our infirmity. *We are no longer under the Law.* We are delivered from the harsh judgment!

THOMAS MERTON, SEASONS OF CELEBRATION, 145–146

THE NEW LAW: LOVE IN CHRIST

In that renewal there is no longer Greek and Jew, circumcised and uncircumcised, barbarian, Scythian, slave and free; but Christ is all and in all!

As God's chosen ones, holy and beloved, clothe yourselves with compassion, kindness, humility, meekness, and patience. Bear with one another and, if anyone has a complaint against another, forgive each other; just as the Lord has forgiven you, so you also must forgive. Above all, clothe yourselves with love, which binds everything together in perfect harmony. And let the peace of Christ rule in your hearts, to which indeed you were called in the one body. And be thankful. Let the word of Christ dwell in you richly; teach and admonish one another in all wisdom; and with gratitude in your hearts sing psalms, hymns, and spiritual songs to God. And whatever you do, in word or deed, do everything in the name of the Lord Jesus, giving thanks to God the Father through him.

COLOSSIANS 3:11–17

PRAYER

I have much to learn. Continue, in your mysterious wisdom, to send teachers into my life, no matter how young or old, who will teach me compassion, kindness, humility, gentleness, and patience. I am a ready student: let my teachers come.

EASTER JOURNAL

How do you experience the strength and peace of the risen Christ?

Wednesday of Easter Week

FREE TO BIND OURSELVES TO CHRIST

*C*hristianity is precisely a liberation from every rigid legal and religious system. This is asserted with such categorical force by St. Paul that we cease to be Christians the moment our religion becomes slavery to "the Law" rather than a free personal adherence by loving faith to the risen and living Christ: "Do you seek justification by the Law…you are fallen from grace…In fact, in Christ Jesus neither circumcision or its absence is of any avail. What counts is faith that expresses itself in love" (Galatians 5:4, 6). And elsewhere he says that the only thing that matters for a Christian is his "new life"—the "new creature" which he has become in Christ (Galatians 6:15).

THOMAS MERTON, *SEASONS OF CELEBRATION*, 147

HE IS OUR PEACE

For he is our peace; in his flesh he has made both groups into one and has broken down the dividing wall, that is, the hostility between us. He has abolished the law with its commandments and ordinances, so that he might create in himself one new humanity in place of the two, thus making peace, and might reconcile both groups to God in one body through the cross, thus putting to death that hostility through it. So he came and proclaimed peace to you who were far off and peace to those who were near; for through him both of us have access in one Spirit to the Father. So then you are no longer strangers and aliens, but you are citizens with the saints and also members of the household of God, built upon the foundation of the apostles and prophets, with Christ Jesus himself as the cornerstone. In him the whole structure is joined together and grows into a holy temple in the Lord; in whom you also are built together spiritually into a dwelling place for God.

EPHESIANS 2:14–22

PRAYER

Un-strange me from myself. Un-alienate my soul to full communion with the Church who mediates the Holy Spirit to the world through your word and sacraments. Un-wall us from one another: let all those who seek you be one. The world is yours and you are ours.

EASTER JOURNAL

Through your experience of this Lent and Easter, how are you a "new creature"?

Thursday of Easter Week

NO LAW BUT CHRIST

The Christian has no Law but Christ. His "Law" is the new life itself which has been given to him in Christ. His Law is not written in books but in the depths of his own heart, not by the pen of man but by the finger of God. His duty is now not just to *obey* but to *live*. He does not have to save himself, he is *saved* by Christ. He must live to God in Christ, not only as one who seeks salvation but as one who *is saved*.

THOMAS MERTON, *SEASONS OF CELEBRATION*, 147

By Grace We All Are Saved

But God, who is rich in mercy, out of the great love with which he loved us even when we were dead through our trespasses, made us alive together with Christ—by grace you have been saved—and raised us up with him and seated us with him in the heavenly places in Christ Jesus, so that in the ages to come he might show the immeasurable riches of his grace in kindness toward us in Christ Jesus. For by grace you have been saved through faith, and this is not your own doing; it is the gift of God—not the result of works, so that no one may boast. For we are what he has made us, created in Christ Jesus for good works, which God prepared beforehand to be our way of life.

EPHESIANS 2:4–10

Prayer

In you, O Lord, I place all my trust. I unashamedly love you. You are my God.

Easter Journal

Have your mind and heart experienced that you have "been saved by grace" through the death and resurrection of Jesus Christ?

Friday of Easter Week

THE COURAGE TO BE FREE

The most important thing that strikes us when we read the Pauline epistles objectively is that most of the things that many sincerely pious Christians worry about are things which do not matter.

We must face the fact that the challenge of this passage (Colossians 2:16–18, 20–23) is too much for many pious Christians. It is much too hot to handle. But if we are risen with Christ, if we are not "enemies of the cross of Christ," and if we believe in Christ's victory over the Law, are going to have to understand words like these and put them into practice in our lives.

THOMAS MERTON, *SEASONS OF CELEBRATION*, 154–155

LOVE GOD TRULY AND THEN DO WHAT YOU WILL

Therefore do not let anyone condemn you in matters of food and drink or of observing festivals, new moons, or sabbaths. These are only a shadow of what is to come, but the substance belongs to Christ. Do not let anyone disqualify you, insisting on self-abasement and worship of angels, dwelling on visions, puffed up without cause by a human way of thinking, and not holding fast to the head, from whom the whole body, nourished and held together by its ligaments and sinews, grows with a growth that is from God.

If with Christ you died to the elemental spirits of the universe, why do you live as if you still belonged to the world? Why do you submit to regulations, "Do not handle, Do not taste, Do not touch"? All these regulations refer to things that perish with use; they are simply human commands and teachings. These have indeed an appearance of wisdom in promoting self-imposed piety, humility, and severe treatment of the body, but they are of no value in checking self-indulgence.

COLOSSIANS 2:16–23

PRAYER

Set me free to love the Lord my God with my whole heart, my whole soul, and my whole strength. Set me free to love my neighbor with my whole heart, my whole soul, and my whole strength. May I yearn for your love as intensely as you yearn for mine.

EASTER JOURNAL

How do you personally understand that, because you love God, you can "do what you want"?

Saturday of Easter Week

SINGING ALLELUIA, GLORIFYING GOD

*I*t is not dutiful observance that keeps us from sin, but something far greater: it is love. And this love is not something which we develop by our own powers alone. It is a sublime gift of the divine mercy, and the fact that we live in the realization of this mercy and this gift is the greatest source of growth for our love and for our holiness.

This gift, this mercy, this unbounded love for God for us has been lavished upon us as a result of Christ's victory. To taste this love is to share in His victory. To realize our freedom, to exult in our liberation from death, from sin and from the Law, is to sing the *Alleluia* which truly glorifies God in this world and the world to come.

THOMAS MERTON, *SEASONS OF CELEBRATION*, 156–157

BENEDICTUS

"Blessed be the Lord God of Israel,
*   for he has looked favorably on his people and redeemed them.*
He has raised up a mighty savior for us
*   in the house of his servant David,*
as he spoke through the mouth of his holy prophets from of old,
*   that we would be saved from our enemies and from the hand*
*   of all who hate us.*
Thus he has shown the mercy promised to our ancestors,
*   and has remembered his holy covenant,*
the oath that he swore to our ancestor Abraham,
*   to grant us that we, being rescued from the hands of our enemies,*
might serve him without fear, in holiness and righteousness
*   before him all our days.*
And you, child, will be called the prophet of the Most High;
*   for you will go before the Lord to prepare his ways,*
to give knowledge of salvation to his people
*   by the forgiveness of their sins.*
By the tender mercy of our God,
*   the dawn from on high will break upon us,*
to give light to those who sit in darkness and in the shadow of death,
*   to guide our feet into the way of peace."*

LUKE 1:68–79

PRAYER

Christ is risen and with him all creation! Light replaces dark, life replaces death, joy replaces sadness, suffering, and fear. Alleluia!

EASTER JOURNAL

What does it mean to you and to your relationship with God and others to share in the resurrection of Christ?

Second Sunday of Easter

CALLED OUT OF DARKNESS

*T*his joy in God, this freedom which raises us in faith and in hope above the bitter struggle that is the lot of man caught between the flesh and the Law, this is the new canticle in which we join with the blessed angels and the saints in praising God.

Let us not then darken the joy of Christ's victory by remaining in captivity and in darkness, but let us declare His power, by living as free men who have been called by Him out of darkness into his admirable light.

THOMAS MERTON, *SEASONS OF CELEBRATION*, 157

Always Stretching Forward Toward Christ

Yet whatever gains I had, these I have come to regard as loss because of Christ. More than that, I regard everything as loss because of the surpassing value of knowing Christ Jesus my Lord. For his sake I have suffered the loss of all things, and I regard them as rubbish, in order that I may gain Christ and be found in him, not having a righteousness of my own that comes from the law, but one that comes through faith in Christ, the righteousness from God based on faith. I want to know Christ and the power of his resurrection and the sharing of his sufferings by becoming like him in his death, if somehow I may attain the resurrection from the dead.

Not that I have already obtained this or have already reached the goal; but I press on to make it my own, because Christ Jesus has made me his own. Beloved, I do not consider that I have made it my own; but this one thing I do: forgetting what lies behind and straining forward to what lies ahead, I press on toward the goal for the prize of the heavenly call of God in Christ Jesus. Let those of us then who are mature be of the same mind; and if you think differently about anything, this too God will reveal to you. Only let us hold fast to what we have attained.

PHILIPPIANS 3:7–16

Prayer

In spring, summer, winter, or fall, let me pray with Saint Anthony of the Desert as I journey toward you, my Lord and my God: "Today I begin again."

Easter Journal

Consider the ways you can declare the power of Christ's victory throughout the Easter season and prepare for the Holy Spirit at Pentecost.